BRENDA COSTIGAN'S
Anything I can do...
COOKBOOK

Favourite Recipes From Her Kitchen

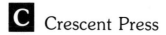 Crescent Press

©Brenda Costigan 1988
Printed November 1988
Reprinted November 1989
Reprinted November 1992
Reprinted December 1993
Reprinted April 1995
Reprinted March 1998
ISBN 0-9514115-0-0

Printed by Printstone Ltd, Unit 5 Cherry Orchard Industrial Est, Dublin 10.

Cover Photograph NEIL MACDOUGALD

My sincere thanks to Jim and Mary O'Donnell for their advice and encouragement, to my daughter Catherine and niece Rebecca O'Donnell for their editing skills, to my sons Peter and David for their back-up services. Special thanks to Neil MacDougald.

For Dick — with love.

Published by Crescent Press (Publishers)
3 Sycamore Crescent
Mount Merrion
Co. Dublin, Ireland.

Contents

Introduction

"When are you going to write a cookery book"? is a question I have been asked more times than I can count. Encouraged by this I have at last gathered together some of my favourite recipes suitable not only for families but also for entertaining friends.

Selecting which recipes to use was not an easy task, but I have included a wide range from soups to desserts, not forgetting my rich Christmas Cake (with the tin of strawberries) which thousands of readers and viewers write to me for each year. All my recipes are family and friend tested! Most of the ingredients I use should be in your kitchen press and those you need to buy won't leave you penniless!

Anyway, I leave you to it and hope that you enjoy making my favourites your favourites.

Brenda Costigan

SOUP AND THINGS!

In the following recipes, the margarine listed can be substituted by olive or vegetable oil (corn, sunflower etc.) Use about 1 tablespoon (22ml) for every 25g (1oz) of margarine.

Delightful meals can be made from most of the recipes in this section. A big bowl of home-made soup, for example, with some bread and cheese — and you're fed! Once you get into the habit, you will discover that lovely soups can be made very simply with both fresh ingredients and leftovers.

STOCK
Anytime you boil a chicken — you have a pot of beautiful stock. Anytime you roast a chicken, put the leftover bones in a pot with a few vegetables and seasoning. Cover with water, boil and then simmer for about 30 minutes — and you get a pot of stock. Even a mugful of soup or stew left over from the day before, added to water will make a stock. When none of these are available use a stock cube!

KNEADED BUTTER (Beurre Marnié)
Fabulous for thickening any liquid at the last minute, for example a soup or stew that you feel is too watery.
> *25 g (1 oz) butter or margarine*
> *25 g (1 oz) flour*
Simply mash these together with a fork on a small plate to make a paste. Drop in small pieces into the liquid. Stir and bring to the boil. Simmer for 2-3 minutes to cook the flour. This amount will thicken 275 ml (½ pt) of liquid.

Soups, on average, will give you approximately 3 servings per 570 ml (1 pt).

Half Home-Made Soup

This is a clever way to get fresh vegetables into soup bowls without changing the flavour of your family's favourite packet soup! You can vary the vegetables depending on what you have available.

1 onion
1 – 2 cloves garlic
1 carrot
1 stick celery
1 potato
50 g (2 oz) margarine
900 ml – 1.1 litre (1½ – 2 pts) water
Salt and freshly ground black pepper
Packet of your favourite soup
Fresh parsley, chopped

Wash, peel and chop the vegetables, then fry them in the margarine (in a saucepan) for a couple of minutes. Pour in the water and add the pepper and salt. Bring to the boil and simmer gently with the lid on until the vegetables are tender (about 15—20 minutes).

Blend the soup powder with enough cold water to make a wet, sloppy paste. Add to the saucepan and stir briskly. Bring to the boil and simmer for 3—5 minutes.

Serve, sprinkled with chopped fresh parsley.

Creamy Vegetable Soup

If your family doesn't like to see the chunks of vegetable in the bowl, simply make the Half Home-Made Soup creamy by "buzzing" the vegetables in a food processor! A few tablespoons of cream can be stirred through the soup.

Note: A potato masher can be used in the absence of a food processor. Sieve the mashed vegetables if necessary to make a fine purée.

Parsley is not just a pretty face — it is a rich source of vitamin C.

Home-Made Vegetable Soup

Home-Made Vegetable Soup is made like the Half Home-Made Soup (page 2), except, you use stock instead of the packet of soup — so follow that recipe....but first read the following points to ensure a good flavour.

— Preferably use a real chicken stock, otherwise use a chicken or vegetable stock cube.
— Fat left over from roasting a chicken can be used instead of the margarine to fry the vegetables.
— Put in generous pinches of mixed herbs or use fresh herbs like bay leaf, thyme and parsley.
— Let your creative imagination run riot (well almost!) in your choice of vegetables. For example pieces of parsnip, cauliflower, leeks and sprouts can also be included.
— If you want the finished soup to have a thicker consistency, add some kneaded butter (page 2).

To eat a wide variety of foods is one of the main guides to healthy eating. Home-made soups are an excellent way to do just that.

Potato Leek and Orange Soup *posh nosh!*

Give a real touch of class to a potato soup by flavouring it with leeks and oranges.

2 medium/large potatoes
1 small onion
1 – 2 cloves garlic
2 sticks celery
1½ large leeks (top and tail them)
50 g (2 oz) margarine
1.1 litre (2 pt) chicken stock
Salt and freshly ground black pepper
Good pinch mixed herbs
To finish:
½ leek, thinly sliced
Juice of 1 large orange
Juicy segments of 1 – 2 oranges
Fresh parsley, chopped

Scrub, scrape and chop the potatoes. Chop the onion, garlic and celery. If the leeks are dirty, wash thoroughly (slitting them if necessary) and slice thinly.

Fry the onion and garlic in the margarine in a large heavy saucepan. When they are soft (not browned), add in the other vegetables and stir around. Pour in the stock, season with salt, pepper and mixed herbs. Bring to the boil and simmer with the lid on, until the vegetables are tender (about 20 minutes). Spoon out the vegetables and "buzz" in a food processor (or mash them). Return to the saucepan. To finish — add the ½ leek (washed and thinly sliced), the orange juice and segments to the soup. Simmer gently to soften leek slightly. Serve with a sprinkling of chopped parsley.

POTATO SOUP
For a straightforward potato soup, omit the orange juice and segments and use only 1 leek in the soup with the other vegetables.

To prepare orange in juicy segments for use in salads and soups. Peel oranges with a sharp knife, removing all the pith and membrane so the flesh just shows. Carefully cut out each segment of orange from **between** the membranes (thin inner skin). A sharp knife is necessary. Work over a bowl to catch the juice that escapes!

French Onion Soup

Traditionally, French onion soup is made with a rich beef stock. Nevertheless, a most tasty soup can be made using stock cubes. For a darker colour, include some tinned consommé.

700 g (1½ lb) onions
2−4 cloves garlic
50 g (2 oz) butter or margarine
2 tablespoons oil
1 teaspoon sugar
Salt and freshly ground black pepper
1 level tablespoon flour
1.75 l (3 pts) water (see note)
2 beef stock cubes
2 bay leaves
To serve (optional):
Spoonful of croûtons and a spoonful of grated cheese per bowl

Slice the onions thinly and chop the garlic. Heat the butter and oil in a large heavy saucepan and fry the onions and garlic for about 10−15 minutes until they turn a nice golden colour — a few of them can be allowed to get very brown. As they fry, add in the sugar, salt and pepper. Next stir in the flour and allow to brown a little. Pour in the water (and consommé). Add the stock cubes and bay leaves. Bring to the boil and simmer, half covered with the lid (to allow the steam escape), for about 45 minutes, by which stage the volume of the soup should be reduced by ¼.

To serve — sprinkle croûtons into piping hot bowls of soup and scatter all over with grated cheese. Grill quickly to melt and brown the cheese.

Note: If you like, substitute two tins of beef consommé (condensed) for 570 ml (1 pt) of the water, and omit 1 stock cube.

Smoked Fish Chowder

Even the name of this recipe is appetizing — straight away, you visualize a chewy tasty soup, which is in fact a meal in itself.

225−450 g (½−1 lb) smoked fish (cod or haddock)

1 medium onion
2 cloves garlic (optional)
1 good sized potato
1 stick celery
1 medium carrot
50 g (2 oz) margarine
2 – 3 rashers, chopped
900 ml (1½ pt) water
1 glass white wine (if you have it handy!)
Sprig parsley and thyme and a bay leaf or, a few pinches of mixed herbs
1 whole clove
Salt and freshly ground black pepper
275 ml (½ pt) milk
Chopped parsley

Put the smoked fish into a bowl and cover with boiling water. Leave it to stand for about 5 minutes while you prepare the vegetables (to reduce the salty flavour). Wash, peel and chop or dice the vegetables. Drain the fish, remove the skin and bones and cut into small chunks. Heat the margarine in a heavy saucepan. Fry the rashers, onion and garlic until tender, then add in the remaining vegetables and fry for a minute or two. Next pour in the water and wine, adding the herbs, the clove, salt, pepper and the fish. Bring to the boil and then simmer the soup gently for about 20 minutes until the vegetables are tender. Remove the bay leaf and the sprigs of parsley and thyme. Add in the milk and the chopped parsley. Taste to see if more salt or pepper is required. Reheat and then serve.

Quick Fish Chowder

A packet of soup is used in this recipe, tomato would be my first choice. The raw fish is cooked in the soup giving it a delicious flavour. This recipe makes the most of a small amount of fish.

1 onion
1 – 2 cloves garlic (optional)
1 carrot
1 potato

1 stick celery
50 g (2 oz) margarine
900 ml – 1.1 litre (1½ – 2 pt) water
Salt and freshly ground black pepper
1 packet soup (tomato or vegetable)
1 fillet white fish, 225 g (8 oz) skinned and cut in chunks
Chopped parsley

Chop or dice the peeled vegetables. First fry the onions and garlic in the margarine until soft. Do this in a heavy saucepan. Put in the other vegetables and toss around for a minute or two. Then add in the water, salt and pepper. Bring to the boil and simmer with the lid on for about 15 minutes until the vegetables are tender. Blend the soup powder with enough water to make a soft paste and whisk it into the contents of the saucepan. Bring to the boil. Now add in the fish. Simmer gently for about 5 minutes until the fish is cooked. Serve sprinkled generously with chopped parsley.

> Centuries ago when the French fishermen returned from a fishing trip, each would throw a portion of his catch into a large copper pot called "la chaudière" so that the villagers could celebrate their home-coming. This is where the name chowder originated.

Garlic Bread

Crush or finely chop about **2 – 4 cloves of garlic**. Mix them into **110 g (4 oz) of butter**. Cut a **French stick** into thick slices. Spread each one generously with this butter. Place slices back into their roll form and wrap in **foil**. Bake in a hot over **(200°C – 400°F – Gas 6)** for about 20 minutes. For variety — a generous pinch of **mixed herbs** can be included in the butter. **A Vienna roll** is also suitable to use.

Croûtons

Cut **4 slices of white or brown bread (1 cm / ½″ thick)** into cubes. Heat about **4 tablespoons of oil** in a pan and fry the cubes in a single layer until golden (don't over-brown them).

Or spread the oil out on a tin and stir the bread cubes in it until they soak it up. Bake in a moderately hot oven **(180°C – 350°F – Gas 4)** for just about 10 minutes. Don't let them burn!

Green Starter (Serves 6)

Light and refreshing and low in calories.

½ **melon**
¼ **cucumber, unpeeled**
2 kiwi fruits, peeled
1 green apple
110 g (4 oz) green grapes
Tablespoon finely chopped leeks
Tablespoon finely chopped parsley
Green mayonnaise

Dice the peeled melon, cucumber, kiwi and apple. Halve and remove pips from the grapes. Mix everything together except the mayonnaise. Chill in the fridge. Before serving, spoon into individual glass dishes (or wine glasses). Spoon a little mayonnaise on each one and sprinkle with a little extra chopped parsley.

To give a special touch: Before filling, dip the rims of the glass dishes into beaten egg white and then into very finely chopped fresh parsley.

Note: The melon, cucumber and apple can be cut into small marble shapes using a Parisienne cutter. They look lovely but this method is a little wasteful, so be more generous with the ingredients.

Green Mayonnaise

3 tablespoons of mayonnaise
½ **avocado pear**
Lemon juice

Peel the avocado, scraping the skin to collect all the dark coloured flesh. Mash to a smooth purée and add to mayonnaise. Flavour with a little lemon juice. Mix well and serve.

Low Fat Chicken Liver Pâté

This pâté is made using cottage cheese instead of the usual butter. It is nice and soft. For a firmer texture, gelatine is added.

| 1 small onion, chopped |
| 2 cloves garlic, chopped |
| 25 g (1 oz) butter |
| 1 tablespoon oil |
| 225 g (8 oz) chicken livers |
| Salt and freshly ground black pepper |
| Pinch mixed herbs |
| 2 tablespoons brandy (or sherry) |
| Generous pinches of ground nutmeg |
| 225 g (8 oz) carton cottage cheese |
| To cover: |
| About 75 g (3 oz) melted butter |
| 2 bay leaves |

Fry the onion and garlic in the butter and oil until soft. Add in the chicken livers and fry until nicely browned. Add the salt, pepper, mixed herbs and brandy. Cook briskly to drive off the alcohol (or you can flambé it — put a match to it — watch your eyebrows!). Put the contents of the pan into the food processor along with the nutmeg and cottage cheese. "Buzz" the lot together until nice and smooth. Turn into a dish. Cover with melted butter (place 2 bay leaves in the centre). Chill before serving.

FIRMER PÂTÉ: Dissolve ½ **packet of gelatine 7 g (¼ oz)** in **2—3 tablespoons of water**. Add it to the pâté when "buzzing" everything together in the food processor.

Note: If a food processor is not available, sieve the cottage cheese and mash or mix everything together to a smooth paste.

Mackerel Dip

You could make this with your eyes closed! Serve as a dip or spread on crackers.

| 1 fillet of smoked mackerel (the peppered ones are very good) |
| 225 g (8 oz) carton cottage cheese |
| Teaspoon mustard or lemon juice |

Remove the skin from the mackerel. Place all the ingredients in the food processor and "buzz" until creamy. Serve in a bowl surrounded by crudités.

CRUDITÉS are raw vegetables cut in narrow fingerlike shapes so they can be used to scoop up the dip with which they are served. Many vegetables are suitable e.g. carrots, celery, cucumber, peppers, radishes, cauliflower and fennel. Choose 3 or 4 with contrasting colours.

Mackerel Mouthfuls

Make the little choux puffs (page 79). Fill them with the mackerel dip. Serve as savouries or as a starter (accompanied with a mini salad).

Mini Quiches

These are marvellous for "standing up" parties! They are a bit fiddley to make but worth all the trouble. I find the wholemeal shortcrust pastry the most effective to use, because it reheats excellently due to its crunchiness. They can be frozen after cooking, then thawed and reheated before serving.

Wholemeal shortcrust pastry using 225 g (8 oz) flour (page 78)
Filling:
8−10 streaky rashers
50 g (2 oz) margarine
1 onion
1−2 cloves garlic (optional)
175 g (6 oz) mushrooms
3−4 tomatoes
3 eggs
50−75 g (2−3 oz) grated cheese, cheddar
Approx. 150 ml (¼ pt) milk
Salt and freshly ground black pepper
1 teaspoon mustard
Chopped fresh parsley

Tin: Two bun trays, 12 hollows in each, the hollows must be shallow ones (about 2.5 cm/1″ deep).

Cooking time: 25—30 minutes **(200°C — 400°F — Gas 6)** in upper half of oven.

Roll out the pastry, cut into circles and place in greased bun trays. Fry the rashers until crispy brown in 15 g (about ½ oz) of the margarine, then chop them finely. Wipe the rasher fat off the pan (it is too salty). Chop the onion, garlic and mushrooms very finely. Put the remaining margarine into the pan and fry the onions and garlic until soft. Lift out onto a plate. Then fry the mushrooms until soft and reduced in bulk. Chop the tomatoes finely. Mix together the eggs, milk, salt, pepper and mustard.

Now comes the fiddley bit! Put a small bit of onion in each pastry case. Do the same with the rashers, mushrooms and tomatoes. Very carefully, pour a little egg mixture into each pastry case — don't fill to the very top as it expands when cooked. Finally, top each one with a little grated cheese.

Bake until nicely golden and well cooked. Serve, sprinkled with chopped parsley.

Curried Mini Meatballs

"Stand-up" party fare! Serve these on wooden cocktail sticks accompanied by chutney flavoured mayonnaise.

1 onion, very finely chopped
2 cloves garlic, crushed
25 g (1 oz) margarine
450 g (1 lb) minced beef, very lean
25 g (1 oz) porridgemeal (rolled oats)
2 rounded dessertspoons curry powder
Salt and freshly ground black pepper
Dessertspoon chutney (mango)
1 large egg
Oil for frying

Fry the onion and garlic in the margarine until soft and add them to the meat together with all the other ingredients. Mix thoroughly and shape into small meatballs (the size of a large marble).

Fry in plenty of hot oil until cooked through. Drain well on kitchen paper. Serve hot. Accompany with a little dish of mayonnaise flavoured with chutney. Guests can dunk their meatballs in it.

Pizza *(Serves 6)*

From the humblest of beginnings in the south of Italy — the pizza has become a world classic. Some versions are topped with everything but the kitchen sink! I include both the quick self raising base and the yeast base so you have a choice.

Yeast base:
275 g (10 oz) strong white or strong wholemeal flour
¼ teaspoon oregano or pizza seasoning
Salt and freshly ground black pepper
½ packet dried yeast, 7 g (¼ oz)
180 ml (just over ¼ pt) water
2 tablespoons oil
or
Self raising base:
275 g (10 oz) self raising flour
¼ teaspoon pizza seasoning or oregano
Salt and freshly ground black pepper
75g (3 oz) margarine
Cold water
Tomato mixture:
1 large onion
2 cloves garlic
50g (2 oz) mushrooms, chopped
Tin of chopped tomatoes
Tablespoon tomato purée
Salt and freshly ground black pepper
Teaspoon sugar
¼ teaspoon oregano or pizza seasoning
25g (1oz) margarine
Optional:
½ courgette, chopped   de-seeded and chopped
½ red or green pepper, de-seeded and chopped
Topping:
175 g (6 oz) cooked ham or salami, chopped
50 – 110 g (2 – 4 oz) grated cheese

Tin: Pizza tin 28 cm (11″) diameter, greased.

Cooking time: About 45 minutes **(200°C — 400°F — Gas 6)**.

To make yeast base:
Strong flour is necessary for successful yeast baking. Mix the flour, seasonings and yeast together in a bowl. Add the water and oil. Mix well together. Turn the dough out onto a lightly floured table and knead very well. Pull and stretch it like the "divil" as this ensures the yeast is well mixed!

Roll out and place in the greased tin. Place the tin into a large, oiled plastic bag and stand in a warm place to allow the dough to rise and become spongy. (Takes 30 — 60 minutes). Remove the bag, cover the dough with the tomato mixture and bake for about 20 minutes. Take out of the oven and cover with the topping of meat and cheese. Return to the oven for another 25 minutes until the cheese is nicely browned.

To make the self raising base:
Mix the flour and seasonings together and rub in the margarine. Add enough cold water to make a softish dough. Roll it out and put into the prepared tin. Don't trim off any extra bits around the edge — just tuck them in. Bake for 10 minutes while you prepare the tomato mixture. Take the tin out of the oven and cover the dough with the tomato mixture. Bake again for another 10 minutes. Then cover the tomato mixture with topping ingredients. Bake for a final 25 minutes or until nicely cooked.

To make tomato mixture:
Thinly slice the onion and garlic and fry in the margarine until soft. Add the mushrooms (also the courgette and pepper if using them). Fry for a few minutes, add in the tinned tomatoes, including juice, and the purée. Season well with salt, pepper, sugar and oregano. Cook gently until the mixture becomes mushy and thick.

Note: You can vary the choice of toppings to suit yourself.

Quiche *(Serves 6-8 or 3-4)*

To say I couldn't survive without my quiche recipe would be an exaggeration but there is no doubt that I find it very handy for many different occasions, from impromptu meals to supper parties.

Shortcrust pastry made using 225 g (8 oz) flour. I prefer wholemeal shortcrust (page 78)

Filling:

175 g (6 oz) streaky rashers
50 g (2 oz) margarine
1 onion, thinly sliced
1 – 2 cloves garlic (optional)
110 g (4 oz) mushrooms, chopped
2 – 3 tomatoes, sliced
2 large eggs (3 for 10″ tin)
About 200 ml (generous ¼ pt) milk
Salt and freshly ground black pepper
Teaspoon mustard
Pinches of ground nutmeg
75 g (3 oz) grated cheese

Tin: 23—25.5 cm (9″ — 10″) sandwich tin **or** 18 cm (7″) sandwich tin and use only half the ingredients for 3—4 servings.

Cooking time: About 40 minutes (about 25 minutes for a smaller one) **(200°C — 400°F — Gas 6)**.

Make pastry, roll out and line the greased tin. Fry the rashers in 15 g (about ½ oz) of the margarine until browned. Chop them and put into the pastry case. Wipe the fat off the pan (it is too salty). Put the remaining margarine in the pan and fry the onions and garlic, then add in the mushrooms. Cook until soft and spoon into the pastry case. Scatter in the tomatoes. Whisk together the eggs and milk and season with salt, pepper, mustard, and pinches of nutmeg. Pour into the pastry case. Sprinkle cheese over the top.

Bake until the filling is well set and golden brown. Don't shorten the baking time as the pastry underneath takes time to cook.

Spinach Quiche

Make as for the Quiche recipe except omit the rashers and tomatoes and use 450 g (1 lb) spinach (cooked and chopped) instead.

Rice Italian Style *(Serves 4-5)*

One of the tastiest ways to cook rice is to simmer it gently in some stock which it absorbs. I mainly use brown rice as it is more nutritious than white rice and it contains some natural fibre.

1 medium onion
2 cloves garlic
2 tablespoons oil or margarine
225 g (8 oz) long grained rice (white or brown)
Salt and freshly ground black pepper
Pinch mixed herbs
570 ml (1 pt) stock (preferably chicken)

Finely chop the onion and garlic and fry in the oil, using a heavy saucepan. When soft, add in the rice and stir for a few minutes over a gentle heat. Season with pepper, salt and mixed herbs. Pour in the stock. Bring to the boil and simmer very gently with the lid on until all the liquid is absorbed (about 20 minutes for white rice and 30 for brown). The rice should be "al dente" as the Italians say which means tender but with a little "bite", not mushy.

If by chance all the stock is absorbed and the rice is not tender, add a little boiling water and continue cooking.

Be careful to keep the heat low so as not to burn the rice.

Green Rice Salad

This looks most attractive, especially if, like me, you love parsley. Use the **Rice Italian Style** recipe (above) with two changes.

(1) Include **2 – 3 sticks celery** (chopped). Add to the rice as it cooks in the saucepan — about 10 minutes before the end of the cooking time.
(2) When cooked and cooled, add **4 tablespoons of finely chopped fresh parsley**.

Chicken or Turkey Risotto

The recipe for Rice Italian Style makes a perfect base into which a variety of chopped meats or vegetables can be added to make a hot or cold meal. If planning to serve it cold, always do the initial frying of the onion in oil, as this does not harden when it gets cold.

To the **Rice Italian style** recipe add the following:—
— Put **110 g (4 oz) sliced mushrooms** into the saucepan with the chopped onion when preparing the rice.
— When the rice is cooked, add **225 g (8 oz) cooked chicken or turkey,** chopped neatly.
— Chopped **cooked vegetables** such as celery, carrot, green beans can be mixed through the rice as well.

Heat everything together in the saucepan if serving hot. Accompany with a tossed salad and crusty bread or garlic bread (page 7).

Speckled Spinach Roulade *(Serves 5-6)*

A savoury Swiss roll that both looks and tastes good. Serve it for lunch, brunch or evening meal. Small portions of it make an impressive starter. It can be made in advance and reheated.

Roulade:
50 g (2 oz) margarine
50 g (2 oz) flour
275 ml (½ pt) milk
3 tablespoons very finely chopped cooked spinach
50 g (2 oz) grated cheese
Salt and freshly ground black pepper
Generous pinches of ground nutmeg
4 large eggs, separated

Filling:
25 g (1 oz) margarine
25 g (1 oz) flour
150 ml (¼ pt) milk
Salt and freshly ground black pepper
110 g (4 oz) mushrooms,chopped and fried
1 – 2 cloves garlic, fried with the mushrooms
Teaspoon lemon juice

Tin: Swiss roll tin 35.5 cm × 23 cm (14″ × 9″). Grease and line with non-stick baking paper (or parchment).

Cooking time: About 25 minutes, placed just above the centre of the oven **(190°C − 375°F − Gas 5)**.

Put the margarine, flour and milk into a saucepan and bring to the boil, stirring briskly with a whisk. Next, stir in the spinach and cheese. Season with salt, pepper and nutmeg. Allow to cool a little. Mix the egg yolks through the mixture. Beat the egg whites until very stiff and stir gently but thoroughly through the mixture. Put into the prepared tin and gently spread it out. Bake until well risen and golden brown.

While it bakes, prepare the filling as follows — put all the ingredients into a saucepan and bring to the boil, stirring briskly with a whisk. Simmer for 2—3 minutes.

Put a piece of greaseproof (or baking) paper on a damp teatowel. Turn the baked roulade onto it. Gently peel off the lining paper. Trim the edges of both long sides of the roulade. Spread the filling over the surface and roll up, using the greaseproof paper to help. Return to the oven for 5—10 minutes to heat through.

Variation: *In the Roulade:* Omit spinach and nutmeg and use **2 tablespoons chopped parsley**. *In the filling* omit mushrooms and use instead **175 g (6 oz) chopped cooked turkey, chicken or fish**.

Apple and Cheese Toasties *(Serves 1-2)*

These make a substantial tasty snack.

1 medium eating apple
50−75 g (2−3 oz) grated cheese (preferably cheddar)
1 slice onion, finely chopped
Salt and freshly ground black pepper
A little mustard
2 slices of buttered toast

Mix all the ingredients together — except the toast, and a little of the cheese. Spread the mixture on the toast and sprinkle the remaining cheese on top. Grill until cheese turns golden. Serve hot, cut in fingers.

Pineapple and Ham Toasties *(Serves 1)*

A real knife and fork snack.

1 slice cooked ham
1 slice buttered toast
A little mustard
1 ring pineapple
25 g (1 oz) grated cheese

Put the slice of ham on the toast. Spread a little mustard on it. Place the pineapple ring on top and cover with grated cheese. Grill until cheese turns golden. Serve hot.

Banana and Rasher Rolls *(Serves 1)*

The sweet flavour of the banana is complemented by the lovely bacon flavour.

1 banana
1 – 2 rashers
1 slice buttered toast

Wrap the rasher round the banana so that the fruit is not visible. (Two rashers may be needed to do this). Secure with wooden cocktail sticks. Grill until rashers are well cooked all over. Serve on the toast.

CHICKEN

Chicken is a very versatile meat. It can be combined successfully with so many different flavours. It has the added advantage of being low in fat and easy to digest — and it is quite reasonable on the pocket.

Chicken is a handy source of tasty stock. The fat left over after roasting a chicken adds super flavour if used to fry vegetables or meat when preparing soups or stews.

Note: Whenever chicken stock is required in a recipe and you have none — simply use 1 chicken stock cube with 570 ml (1 pt) water.

"Souper" Chicken *(Serves 5-6)*

This recipe is "souper" in more ways than one! It is a real "bung in the oven" job, yet the resulting flavour is delicious. The chicken is served in its lovely soupy juices.

1 roasting chicken
1 tin or packet of soup (chicken or vegetable)
Salt and freshly ground black pepper

Cooking time: about 1½ hours **(190°C — 375°F — Gas 5)**

If using a packet of soup, make up in the usual way, but only use 400 ml (¾ pt) water. Put the chicken in a casserole and pour the soup over it. Season with salt and pepper. Cover with lid and cook in the centre of the oven until tender.

Chicken Paprika *(Serves 5-6)*

This dish has a rich, warm, colour which is most attractive and it reheats well. The paprika has a mild flavour.

1 large chicken or chicken portions
110 g (4 oz) margarine
2 onions, chopped
2—4 cloves garlic, chopped
1—2 heaped teaspoons paprika
50 g (2 oz) flour
570—900 ml (1—1½ pt) chicken stock
1 tin tomatoes

2 tablespoons tomato purée

1 glass wine (optional)

1 stick celery, sliced

1 red pepper, de-seeded and sliced

110 g (4 oz) button mushrooms, sliced

Salt and freshly ground black pepper

Mixed herbs

Teaspoon sugar

½ - 1 teaspoon cayenne pepper (hot) (optional)

Cooking time: In a saucepan — about 1 hour
In the oven — about 1½ hours **(180°C — 350°F — Gas 4)**

Fry the chicken in half the margarine until golden brown on all sides. Then transfer to a saucepan or casserole. Fry the onions and garlic until soft and add in the paprika. Fry for a few minutes and then put in with the chicken. Melt the remaining margarine in the pan and add in the four. Cook for 2-3 minutes, then stir in the stock (it is quicker to whisk it in). Bring to the boil and pour over the chicken. Next empty the tin of tomatoes over the chicken along with the purée, wine, celery, red pepper, and mushrooms. Season with salt, pepper, mixed herbs and the sugar and cayenne pepper.

Put the covered casserole into the centre of the oven and cook until the chicken is tender. If using a saucepan, first bring it to the boil and then simmer very gently, with the lid on, until tender.

Serve with noodles, rice or potatoes and a nice green vegetable. If you'd like the juices to be thicker, use kneaded butter (page 2).

Coq au Vin *(Serves 4-6) posh nosh!*

I am sure that the ingenious French housewife, who devised this delicious recipe to cook her old hen, never realized it would become a world famous recipe. The cooked dish has a nice beige/brown colour.

1 large chicken, cut in portions

4 rashers, smoked if possible

2 tablespoons of oil

50 g (2 oz) butter (or margarine)

175 g (6 oz) button mushrooms

| 225 g (8 oz) shallots or small onions |
| 2 cloves garlic (or more!), chopped |
| 1 teaspoon sugar |
| 3 tablespoons brandy (optional) |
| 570 ml (1 pt) red wine |
| 400 ml (¾ pt) chicken stock |
| Salt and freshly ground black pepper |
| ½ teaspoon of mixed herbs *or* use fresh parsley, thyme and bay leaf |
| 40 g (1½ oz) butter |
| 40 g (1½ oz) flour |
| Chopped fresh parsley |

Cooking time: In a saucepan about 1 hour
In the oven about 1½ hours **(180°C — 350°F — Gas 4)**

Chop and fry the rashers in the oil and butter. Transfer them to a saucepan or casserole. Next fry the chicken until golden brown all over and put with the rashers. Lightly fry the shallots and garlic, sprinkling the sugar over them. When golden brown, add to chicken along with all the remaining ingredients — except the butter, flour and chopped parsley. Bring to the boil and simmer gently with the lid on until tender. If cooking in the oven, place on centre shelf, put the lid on the casserole and cook until chicken is tender. Mash the butter and flour together on a plate with a fork. Drop this paste in small pieces into the cooking liquid. Cook for about 10 minutes, stirring or shaking the saucepan or casserole occasionally. Sprinkle with chopped parsley when serving.

Creamy mashed potatoes and a green vegetable are delicious with this dish.

Note: if you do have a boiling fowl (old hen!) allow an extra hour of cooking time.

| Butter burns very easily! To prevent this, add an equal amount of oil. |

Crispy Chicken Breasts with Orange Sauce *(Serves 4)*

Chicken breasts dipped in egg and oatmeal are delightfully crunchy when fried. White sauce flavoured with orange juice makes the perfect accompaniment.

1 tablespoon flour
Salt and freshly ground black pepper
4 chicken breasts
1 egg, beaten
50 g (2 oz) porridgemeal (rolled oats) (see note)
Margarine or oil
275 ml (½ pt) white sauce (page 67)
Juice 1 large orange
1 spring onion (scallion) or ¼ leek

Season the flour with salt and pepper and dip the chicken breasts in it. Then dip into the beaten egg and finally in the porridgemeal. Gently fry them in hot margarine until golden brown and cooked through.

Meanwhile, make up the white sauce and add the orange juice and the neatly chopped spring onion. Simmer gently for a couple of minutes and serve with the chicken. Decorate with slices of orange.

Note: The porridgemeal can be "buzzed" in the food processor if a finer textured coating is preferred.

Chicken in White Wine (or Cider) (Serves 4) posh nosh!

This is delicious! Not only that, but it won't spoil if made in advance, simply reheat gently in the lovely creamy sauce. Double the quantities for 8 people.

1 – 2 cloves garlic, chopped
½ medium onion, finely chopped
50 g (2 oz) margarine (or butter and oil)
4 chicken breasts (or portions)
½ bottle white wine (not sweet) or 350 ml (almost ¾ pt) cider
Salt and freshly ground black pepper
¼ chicken stock cube (see note)
15 g (about ½ oz) butter or margarine
15 g (about ½ oz) flour
2 – 3 tablespoons of cream

Use a large frying pan or a heavy based saucepan that will fit the chicken breasts side by side.

Fry the garlic and onions gently in the margarine until soft but not browned. Then add in the chicken breasts and fry them until they turn white. Now pour in the wine. Season with salt and pepper and the ¼ stock cube. Bring to the boil, cover with a lid and simmer very gently until the chicken is cooked, (about 20 minutes). Lift out the breasts and keep to one side. Boil the cooking juices briskly to reduce them by at least one third. Meanwhile, mash the butter and flour together using a fork. Drop this paste into the cooking juices in little pieces and whisk briskly. Bring to the boil. Add in the cream and the chicken breasts. Season if necessary. Reheat gently.

Note: If, by chance, you have 1—2 tablespoons of fat free roasting juices from a chicken in your fridge — use them istead of the stock cube!

ALCOHOL

In almost all recipes where wine or other alcohol is used, the dish must be thoroughly cooked or its flavour and digestibility will be impaired. If alcohol is flambéd (set on fire) or if it is cooked in the dish for over an hour it is alright. Otherwise the dish/sauce should be cooked briskly to reduce volume of liquid by about one third.

Note to teetotallers: all alcohol is driven off during cooking leaving only the flavour!

Boiling and Roasting Notes

When boiling a chicken, don't be over generous with the water, otherwise the resulting stock will be too weak. As well as an onion, carrot and stick of celery, also add a few cloves of garlic to the water. Season well with salt, freshly ground black pepper and mixed herbs. Boiling takes about 30 minutes cooking time for every 450 g (1 lb) of chicken weight.

When roasting a chicken, spread butter or margarine generously over the breast. Season with salt and freshly ground black pepper. Sprinkle chopped onion, chopped garlic, grated lemon rind and some mixed herbs over it. Cover loosely with foil and roast in a hot oven **(200°C — 400°F — Gas 6)** allowing about 30 minutes for every 450 g (1 lb) chicken weight. Remove foil for last half hour to allow browning.

Some fresh herbs (thyme, parsley, bay leaf) placed in chicken cavity during roasting gives good flavour.

24

Chicken Sycamore *(Serves 4-6)*

This is a nice way to serve a chicken after boiling it. It gives the illusion of lots of chicken.

1 boiled chicken
50 g (2 oz) margarine
50 g (2 oz) flour
900 ml (1½ pt) chicken stock
Teaspoon mustard (a nice grainy one) *or* juice of ½ lemon
Salt and freshly ground black pepper
Dessertspoon chopped parsley

Divide the chicken into portions or else cut all the flesh into small chunks — discarding bones and skin. This way no one knows which is breast or leg meat!

Put the margarine, flour and chicken stock into a saucepan and bring to the boil, stirring briskly with a whisk all the time. Add in the mustard or lemon juice, salt and pepper, chopped parsley and the chicken pieces. Simmer gently for 5—10 minutes. Serve.

Chicken (or Turkey) Pie *(Serves 4-5)*

Cooked chicken or turkey is chopped and put in a tasty sauce, then baked in a pastry case — lovely for a party. Double the ingredients for 8 servings.

225 – 350 g (8 – 12 oz) cooked chicken or turkey
50 g (2 oz) margarine
50 g (2 oz) flour
1 clove garlic, crushed
275 ml (½ pt) chicken stock
Salt and freshly ground black pepper
Juice ½ lemon
75 g (3 oz) sliced mushrooms, lightly fried
Half of 350 g (12 oz) packet of frozen puff pastry.

Tin: Sandwich tin 21.5 cm (8½″) diameter, greased. For double quantities, use Swiss roll tin 32 cm × 23 cm (12½″ × 9″).

Cooking time: About 30 minutes. (About 45 minutes for double quantities).
(200°C — 400°F — Gas 6)

Cut the chicken into small chunks. Put the margarine, flour, garlic and chicken stock into a saucepan. Bring to the boil, stirring briskly with a whisk. Add salt, pepper, lemon juice, the mushrooms and chopped chicken. Simmer for 2—3 minutes.

Divide the pastry in half (slightly unevenly!). Roll out the larger bit and use to line the tin. Pour in the sauce mixture. Fold the edges of the pastry back over the filling. Wet exposed edges with water. Cover the pie with the remaining (rolled out) pastry. Press edges together to seal. Pierce a few holes in the top. Bake until pastry is golden brown and well cooked.

Chicken (or Turkey) Pancakes *(Serves 4-6)*

The same chicken (or turkey) sauce filling used in the chicken pie recipe is suitable as a filling for pancakes.

Make pancakes using recipe below.

Divide the sauce between them and roll or fold up the pancakes. Place in a greased dish, cover with greased paper and heat in oven for about ½ hour **(180°C — 350°F — Gas 4)**.

Variation: Omit the mushrooms, and put in a little cooked spinach in each pancake with the chicken sauce.

Pancakes

Use all white flour or half white and half wholemeal to make the pancakes. This amount of batter will give you 8 pancakes (about 23 cm/9″ in diameter).

110 g (4 oz) flour
2 eggs
275 ml (½ pt) milk
Tablespoon oil

To make pancakes in a food processor or liquidizer:

Simply put in all the ingredients and "buzz" for about 1 minute until smooth. Leave batter to stand for 30 minutes.

To make pancakes by hand:

Put the flour into a bowl and make a large well (hole) in the centre. Drop the eggs into this hole with a little of the milk. Stir the eggs and milk with a wooden spoon, *inside* the hole, without touching the flour around the sides! The liquid will gradually draw in the flour a little at a time. As the liquid thickens add a little more of the milk. Stir until all the flour has been drawn in. Then add the remaining milk. Beat for a few minutes. Leave to stand for 30 minutes.

To fry: transfer batter to a jug and pour about 2 large tablespoons of it onto a hot, lightly greased pan. Fry until brown on both sides. Continue until all pancakes are made.

If made in advance, stack pancakes on a plate, cover and store in the fridge. Pancakes can be frozen, separated from each other with foil or plastic.

Chicken Curry *(Serves 4-6)*

The curry sauce has a lovely chunky texture but if you'd prefer it smooth, "buzz" in food processor after cooking.

4 – 6 portions of chicken (raw or cooked)
Sauce:
50 g (2 oz) margarine
1 onion, finely chopped
2 cloves garlic, chopped
2 – 4 level tablespoons curry powder
1 rounded tablespoon flour
570 ml (1 pt) chicken stock
1 carrot, very thinly sliced
1 small cooking apple, diced or grated
1 teaspoon grated root ginger (optional)
1 dessertspoon mango chutney
Salt and freshly ground black pepper

Sauce: Melt the margarine and fry the onion and garlic until soft. Add in the curry powder and cook for a minute or two. Next, stir in the flour, cook gently for about 1 minute. Remove from the heat and pour in stock. Whisk briskly and add in all the remaining ingredients. Bring sauce to the boil, constantly stirring it.

If using cooked chicken portions (or chunks), simply add to sauce and simmer very gently with the lid on until heated through (about 15 minutes).

If using raw chicken portions, fry them in a little margarine to brown them. Transfer to an ovenproof dish, pour the curry sauce on top, cover with a lid (or foil) and cook in the centre of the oven for about 1 hour, until chicken is tender **(180°C — 350°F — Gas 4)**. The juice from the cooking chicken gives even greater flavour to the sauce.

For a smooth sauce, lift out chicken onto warm serving dish, "buzz" sauce in food processor. Reheat quickly in a saucepan and spoon over chicken.

Accompany curry with plain boiled rice and little bowls each containing a different ingredient, such as sliced tomatoes, coconut or toasted nuts, pineapple chunks, sliced bananas, chutney, cucumber in natural yoghurt or whatever else you fancy!

Terrine of Chicken
(Serves 10 as a starter — serves 6 as a main dish)

If you are looking for something a little special, you might be tempted to try this. It makes a lovely starter or it can be served as a main dish with a salad.

1 small chicken
450 g (1 lb) lean bacon (in a piece)
½ bottle white wine *or* 350 ml (nearly ¾ pt) of cider
2 cloves garlic
Pinch mixed herbs
2 bay leaves
Salt and freshly ground black pepper
2 tablespoons of chopped fresh parsley

Divide the chicken into 4—6 sections. Remove fat from the bacon (optional), cut into big chunks. Put all the ingredients except the parsley into a saucepan and cover with a lid. Bring to the boil. Simmer very gently until meat is very tender (about 1½ hours).

Lift out meat. Remove all flesh from the chicken bones and discard the skin. Finely chop the chicken and bacon (this can be done in a food processor). I like to "buzz" some of the meats and chop the rest so there is a combination of smooth and chunky. Mix 150 ml (¼ pt) of the cooking liquid into the meat mixture along with the chopped parsley. Put into loaf tin 23 cm × 12.5 cm (9″ × 5″) or a dish, while still warm. Smooth out evenly and chill.

Special finish: To give a nice green top to the terrine.

½ packet gelatine 7 g (¼ oz)

150 ml (¼ pt) cooking liquid

2 tablespoons finely chopped parsley

Dissolve the gelatine in the cooking juices and add in the parsley. Pour into the loaf tin or dish. Put in ice box or freezer to set quickly. Then spoon in meat mixture and chill.

Dip tin/dish in very hot water for 60 seconds, then turn out onto plate.

Chicken Stir Fry *(Serves 2)*

Stir frying is a very quick method of cooking. This particular combination of ingredients is very fresh and attractive.

---

2 chicken breasts

1 courgette, about 175 g (6 oz)

2 scallions or ½ leek

1 firm tomato, skinned

1 – 2 tablespoons oil

50 g (2 oz) cashew nuts (see note)

1 tablespoon finely chopped onion

Teaspoon chopped parsley

Salt and freshly ground black pepper

Cut the chicken into neat fingerlike pieces. Divide the courgette in three and slit each section into 4 or 6 fingerlike pieces. Cut the scallions (or piece of leek) into long skinny pieces. Divide the tomato into eights.

Heat the oil in the pan, fry the nuts until golden and lift out. Next fry the chicken pieces until lightly golden and then add in the onion and courgette. Stir fry gently until vegetables are "bite" tender, by which time the chicken will be cooked through. Add in the scallions, fry for a minute and then add in tomato and parsley. Season with salt and pepper, fry gently to heat, add in the nuts and serve as soon as possible.

Note: Cashew nuts can be substituted by whatever kind you have handy. For a special treat, use pine kernels — be careful, they brown quickly.

Chicken in Lemon and Honey Sauce *(Serves 3)*

Quick and simple.

---

3 chicken breasts

2 tablespoons of oil

1 onion, thinly sliced

2 cloves garlic, crushed

Grated rind and juice ½ lemon

200 ml (⅓ pt) water

1 rounded teaspoon cornflour

1 teaspoon honey

Salt and freshly ground black pepper

Tablespoon finely chopped parsley

Fry the chicken breasts until golden brown. Add in the onion, garlic and lemon rind. Fry until they are soft. Blend the water and cornflour, then add to the pan with the lemon juice, honey, salt and pepper. Bring to boil and then simmer gently (with a lid on) for about 15 minutes.

Sprinkle with the parsley and serve.

FISH

Fish is always my first choice whenever I eat out! The speed at which fish can be cooked is a great convenience. Nutritionally it is very attractive with its low fat content.

Home-Made Fish Fingers *(Goujons)*

Dipping fish in egg and breadcrumbs makes a small piece of fish more substantial to eat. **Use thin fillets of fish,** such as whiting, plaice or tail ends of cod and haddock. Allow about **110 – 175 g (4 – 6 oz) per person.** Cut the fillets into fingerlike strips diagonally across the fillet, thus giving you longer fingers!

Dip each one in **flour,** then in **beaten egg** and then in **well seasoned fine breadcrumbs.** Fry until golden and cooked through. Drain. Serve with **mayonnaise** flavoured with **chopped onion, parsley and gherkins.**

Note: Goujons of cod (or whatever fish was used) is the French name for this dish. Sounds posh!

Curried Fish *(Serves 4)*

A substantial dish.
Make up the **curry sauce** included in the chicken curry recipe (page 27). Leave out the chicken! Put **1 lb thick fillets of white fish** into a greased ovenproof dish. Pour the curry sauce on top. Cover with foil and bake for about 30 minutes. **(200°C – 400°F – Gas 6).** Serve with rice and chutney.

Note: Instead, the fish can be added to the saucepan of curry sauce and cooked in it for about 7 – 10 minutes.

Country Vegetable Fish Bake *(Serves 4)*

The vegetables in this recipe are cooked until just tender before being added to the fish. This is a lovely fresh tasting, low calorie dish.

1 carrot
1 onion
1 potato
2 sticks celery
1 leek

50 g (2 oz) margarine

Salt and freshly ground black pepper

150 ml (¼ pt) water

1 bay leaf

Tablespoon finely chopped parsley

450 – 700 g (1 – 1½ lb) white fish fillets (thick ones)

Cooking time: about 15 minutes **(200°C – 400°F – Gas 6)**

Dice the carrot, onion and potato. Thinly slice the celery and leek. Heat the margarine in a big saucepan and fry the onion until soft. Then add in the carrot, potato and celery. Season with salt and pepper and cook gently for about 5 minutes. Next add the leek, water, bay leaf and parsley. Simmer together, with the lid on, for about 10 minutes until the vegetables are just tender.

Grease an oven proof dish and place fish fillets side by side. Pour the piping hot vegetable mixture on top. Cover very loosely with foil and bake until fish is cooked. Serve with garlic bread or wholemeal scones, or vegetables of your choice.

GRILLED FISH

For the calorie conscious person, grilled fish is a good choice. I always lay a piece of foil on the grill tray, lightly brushed with oil or butter, on which I place the fish. This makes it much easier to lift off.

Rainbow Trout with Thyme

Try saying that in a hurry!
A generous **sprig of fresh thyme** placed inside the cavity of the cleaned out **Rainbow trout** gives it good flavour. Spread a little **butter or oil** over the skin, season with **salt and freshly ground black pepper** and grill on each side until cooked through. Flavour a little **mayonnaise** with **chopped thyme** to serve with it.

Fish Pie (Serves 4-5)

The pastry I like to use for this fish pie is wholemeal shortcrust. The crunchy texture of the pastry contrasts beautifully with the smooth fish sauce.

Wholemeal shortcrust pastry using 225 g (8 oz) flour (page 78) or frozen puff pastry 175 g (6oz).

Filling:

450 g (1 lb) white fish fillets

275 ml (½ pt) milk

Salt and freshly ground black pepper

Pinch mixed herbs or a bay leaf

1 slice onion

1 leek, well washed and sliced

40 g (1½ oz) *each* margarine and flour

25 g (1 oz) grated cheese

Teaspoon of mustard

Tin: 21.5 cm. (8½") sandwich tin, greased.

Cooking time: about 35 minutes **(200°C — 400°F — Gas 6)**

First make the filling. Put the fish, milk, salt, pepper, mixed herbs, slice of onion and chopped leeks (or mushrooms) into a saucepan. Bring to the boil and simmer, to barely cook the fish. Lift out fish and leeks. Discard skin from the fish. Using a fork, mash together the margarine and flour on a little plate. Drop this paste into the milk and bring to the boil, stirring briskly with a whisk. Add the grated cheese and mustard and simmer for 2—3 minutes. Cover surface of sauce with foil while you prepare the pastry. Roll out half the pastry to line the greased tin. Put the fish and leek into the pastry case and cover with the sauce. Roll out the remaining pastry and place on top, trimming to fit. Wet and press edges firmly so they stick together. Pierce a few holes in the top. Brush with beaten egg if you like. Bake until the pastry is well cooked. Serve with a salad, or vegetables of your choice.

Note: Lightly fried mushrooms (110 g/4 oz) can be used instead of the leek.

"Souper" Fish *(Serves 4-6)*

This is a real "bung in the oven" dish!

450 — 700 g (1 — 1½ lb) white fish fillets

Tin condensed mushroom soup (or asparagus)

150 ml (¼ pt) milk

Salt and freshly ground black pepper

25 g (1 oz) grated cheddar cheese

Cooking time: about 30 minutes **(200°C — 400°F — Gas 6)**

Place the fish in a single layer in a greased oven proof dish. Mix the tin of soup with the milk and pour over the fish. Season with salt and pepper and sprinkle grated cheese on top. Bake until cooked through and lightly browned on top. Serve with wedges of lemon.

Smoked Fish Bake *(Serves 4)*

The egg and milk set like a custard and the top browns deliciously.

350 — 450 g (¾ — 1lb) smoked cod or haddock

25g (1 oz) margarine

1 small onion, chopped

50 — 110 g (2 — 4 oz) mushrooms, sliced

2 large eggs

275 ml (½ pt) milk

Salt and freshly ground black pepper

Teaspoon of mustard.

Cooking time: 45 minutes approx. **(180°C — 350°F — Gas 4)**

Pour boiling water over the fish in a bowl. Leave for 10 minutes. Drain and skin the fish, cut in big chunks and place side by side in greased ovenproof dish. Melt the margarine and fry the onion until soft. Then add in the mushrooms and fry lightly. Spoon them over the fish. Whisk the eggs and milk together and season with salt, pepper and mustard. Then pour over the fish.

Bake in the centre of the oven until the custard is well set and golden brown.

Extra touch: Sprinkle some grated cheese on the top, halfway through the cooking time.

Variation: Use white fish fillets instead of smoked.

Tuna Burgers *(Serves 4-5)*

The meaty flavour of tuna fish is perfect for these burgers. I much prefer the tuna tinned in brine rather than oil, it has a lighter flavour and is lower in calories.

Tin of tuna fish, drained 200 g (7 oz)
½ small onion, chopped finely
2 small sticks celery, chopped
50 g (2 oz) breadcrumbs
Tablespoon lemon juice
1 egg
2 – 3 tablespoons mayonnaise
Salt and freshly ground black pepper
Oil or margarine, to fry
4 – 5 toasted baps

Mix all the ingredients (except the oil and baps) together in a bowl. Heat the oil or margarine in a pan. Place tablespoonfuls of the mixture onto the pan. Flatten them into round shapes about 2 cm (¾") thick while on the pan. Fry gently until golden brown on both sides. Drain and serve hot in toasted baps with lettuce and mayonnaise.

Plaice in Cream *(Serves 1 or more!)*

Any white fish is suitable for this dish, but plaice is my preference.

Per serving:
175 – 225 g (6 – 8 oz) fillet of plaice
25 g (1 oz) margarine
Dessertspoon chopped onion
50 g (2 oz) mushrooms, sliced
Salt and freshly ground black pepper
2 tablespoons fresh cream
Pinches of ground nutmeg

Melt the margarine and fry the onion until soft, then add in the mushrooms and fry until nearly golden. Make space on the pan and put in the fillet of fish, skin side upwards. Fry for a minute or two, then turn over. Season with salt and pepper and pour in the cream. Simmer gently until the fish is cooked (about 5 minutes) and all the flavours mingle together.

Milky Cod *(Serves 3-4)*

Quick and easy. Fish fillets are poached in milk, which is then thickened to make a sauce.

450 g (1 lb) cod fillets (thick ones)
400 ml (¾ pt) milk
1 slice onion
Salt and freshly ground black pepper
25 g (1 oz) *each* margarine and flour
Tablespoon of chopped fresh parsley

Cut large fish fillets into individual portions and place in a saucepan. Choose a wide based one, (it's easier to lift out the cooked fish). Pour in the milk and add the onion, salt and pepper. Cover with a lid, bring to the boil and simmer gently until fish is cooked. This takes about 7—10 minutes, depending on the thickness of the fish.

Lift out the fish onto a hot serving plate. Use a fork to mash the margarine and flour together on a plate. Drop this paste in little pieces into the milk. Bring to the boil, stirring briskly with a whisk. Add in the parsley and more salt and pepper if necessary. Simmer for 2—3 minutes. Pour over the fish and serve.

Baked Salmon

A delicious way to cook salmon, whether in cutlets or whole, is to wrap it in foil and to allow it to cook in its own juices. If you are baking a whole salmon, the traditional way is to leave the head on, but in no way is this obligatory. Trim off any fins and be sure the body cavity is thoroughly clean. Rinse it under running water. Do not remove scales as they protect the very fine skin.

1 salmon cutlet per person
***or* 1 whole salmon, (about 2.3 kg (5lb),**
Salt and freshly ground black pepper
butter or margarine

Butter the centre of a large piece of foil. Place the cutlets or the whole fish on it. Scatter a few little pieces of butter on top and season with salt and freshly ground black pepper. Close the foil right over the salmon. Don't skimp on the foil as the salmon needs protection to keep the moisture in. Bake in the centre of a moderate oven **(180°C — 350°F — Gas 4)**. Allow about 15 minutes cooking time for every 450 g (1lb) salmon being cooked plus an extra 15 minutes at the end. Test if properly cooked by inserting a knife between the flesh and the back bone. They should separate easily. If not, cook for longer. Lift cooked salmon onto hot serving dish. Remove the skin, keep warm.

SAUCE

You can serve the cooking juices as they are or they can be "dressed up" as follows.

To every 3 tablespoons cooking juices add:
1 teaspoon kneaded butter (page 2)
1 teaspoon lemon juice
1 — 2 tablespoons cream
Salt and freshly ground black pepper

Put the juices, kneaded butter and lemon juice in a little saucepan and stir briskly with a whisk until they boil (for 1-2 minutes). Add the cream, salt and pepper, heat gently and pour over fish.

MEAT

In the following recipes, the margarine listed can be substituted by olive or vegetable oil (corn, sunflower etc.) Use about 1 tablespoon (22ml) for every 25g (1oz) of margarine.

In this section, I include some of my favourite stew recipes. I find these very handy on days when everyone comes in at different times. Individual portions can so easily be heated up. All stews benefit from a few hours standing as it allows the flavours to mingle together.

Also I include some of my family's favourite minced meat recipes. When I fry minced meat preparing a dish, I always tilt the pan sideways to let the excess fat drain down and then remove it.

Hungarian Goulash *(Serves 4-6)*

The name goulash is derived from the Hungarian word for herdsman. This hearty dish helped him to endure the severe weather conditions which prevailed! Paprika with its mild flavour gives a wonderful rich colour to this dish.

700 g (1½ lb) stewing beef (rib or round)
75 g (3 oz) margarine
450 g (1 lb) onions, sliced
2 cloves of garlic, chopped
1 – 2 heaped teaspoons paprika
1 tablespoon flour
Generous 570 ml (1 pt) of stock, beef or chicken
1 tin tomatoes, including juice
Glass red wine (if handy!)
2 carrots, chopped
1 stick celery, chopped
1 red pepper, de-seeded and chopped
¼ teaspoon caraway seeds
Salt and freshly ground black pepper

Cooking time: In a saucepan — about 1½ hours
In the oven — about 2 hours **(180°C — 350°F — Gas 4)**

Cut the meat into bite sized chunks, discarding all fat and grizzle. Fry the meat in two or three lots until browned all over. Transfer to a saucepan or casserole. Fry the onions and garlic until soft. Add the paprika to the onions and fry for a minute or two, then add in the flour. Cook, stirring for another minute or two and then stir in the stock. Bring to the boil and add to the meat. Pour the tin of tomatoes and the wine into the meat. Add in the vegetables, salt, pepper and the caraway seeds.

If using the saucepan: bring to the boil and then simmer gently with the lid on until meat is tender.

If using the casserole: cover the casserole with the lid and cook in the oven until the meat is tender.

Serving suggestion: Put a spoonful of natural yoghurt or dairy soured cream on each serving. Accompany with noodles, rice or potatoes.

Creamy Irish Stew *(Serves 4-6)*

Traditional Irish stew is difficult to make successfully without the strongly flavoured mutton available in times past. Instead, I love to make this creamy version. Don't omit the whole cloves as they add a special touch to the flavour.

700 g (1½ lb) stewing lamb or gigot chops
2 carrots, sliced
2 onions, quartered
Pinch mixed herbs
2 whole cloves — the apple tart kind!
Sprig of parsley
Water
Salt and freshly ground black pepper
50 g (2 oz) each of flour and margarine
110g (4 oz) frozen peas, thawed
Tablespoon lemon juice or teaspoon mustard
3 tablespoons cream or natural yoghurt (optional)
Chopped fresh parsley

Stage I: Cut the lamb into bite size pieces. If using chops leave them whole. Put the meat in a saucepan with the carrots, onions, herbs, cloves and sprig of parsley. Cover with cold water and season well with salt and pepper. Bring to the boil and simmer gently with the lid on until the meat is tender (about 1 hour).

Have you time to let the stew sit for a while and let the excess fat solidify on top and be easily removed? If not, see the tip on page 42.

Stage 2: If you have used the chops, lift them out and cut them into bite size pieces, discarding the fat and bone. (There is far less waste if this is done after cooking rather than before). Put the margarine and flour in a saucepan with 900 ml (1½ pts) of the cooking liquid (strained). Bring to the boil, whisking all the time. Add the meat, carrots, onions and the peas. Season to taste with lemon juice or mustard and extra salt and pepper if necessary. Add the cream or yoghurt. Simmer gently to heat thoroughly. Serve scattered with plenty of chopped fresh parsley.

Note: Spare cooking liquid makes a delicious stock for a vegetable soup.

Quick Creamy Irish Stew

This is a great family dish, it is the same as the other Creamy Irish Stew except that you use a packet of country vegetable soup to thicken the cooking liquid instead of the margarine and flour.

Follow the directions for stage 1, except leave out the whole cloves. If you like, include a potato or two with the other vegetables. When the meat is tender, blend the soup powder with enough cold water to make a soft paste. Add this gradually to the saucepan of meat and vegetables together with the peas (if using them). Bring to the boil and simmer for about 5 minutes. Tasty, isn't it?

Note: Serve spare juices as soup.

To remove melted fat from the surface of soups or stews: Using clean paper towels, one at a time, allow them to touch the surface of the liquid before quickly lifting off. The paper towel will have removed some of the fat. Repeat process until all the fat disappears.

Belgian Beef Casserole *(Serves 4-6)*

Beef, onions and beer are the main ingredients in this traditional rib-tickling stew. I like to include lots of carrots as well because they are low in both cost and calories, and blend in well with the slightly sweet flavour . Don't be worried about alcohol content — it is all driven off during cooking.

3 large onions
2–3 cloves garlic
75 g (3 oz) margarine

2 teaspoons sugar

700 g (1½ lb) lean stewing beef (rib or round)

1 tablespoon flour

570 ml (1 pt) beef stock

275 ml (½ pt) beer or lager

1 teaspoon vinegar

¼ teaspoon mixed herbs

450 g (1 lb) carrots, sliced

Salt and freshly ground black pepper

To finish: (optional) slices of French bread and mustard

Cooking time: In a saucepan — about 1½ hours
In the oven — about 2 hours **(180°C — 350°F — Gas 4)**

Fry the sliced onions and garlic in the margarine until soft. Add in the sugar as you fry. Transfer to saucepan or casserole. Cut meat into bite size chunks and fry in two or three lots until browned all over. Add to the onions.

Mix the flour with the tablespoon of fat that should be left in the pan (if necessary, add extra). Cook until the mixture browns lightly. Remove from the heat and stir in the stock or, better still, whisk it in. Bring to the boil and pour into the meat along with the beer, vinegar, herbs, carrots, salt and pepper. Cook in the saucepan or casserole (with lids) until meat is tender. Leave to stand for a few hours to allow flavours mellow. Reheat when required.

To finish: If stew has been cooked in a saucepan, transfer it to an ovenproof dish. Spread the slices of French bread with mustard and place them, mustard side down, all over the top of the stew. Cook in a hot oven **(200°C — 400°F — Gas 6)** until bread is golden and crisp. Underneath the bread will be deliciously soft and juicy.

> When browning chunks of meat, don't put too much in the pan at one time as this lowers the heat of the pan and the meat goes all juicy.

Pork and Mustard Stew *(Serves 4-6)*

No — it's not a misprint! The tablespoon of mustard powder listed in the ingredients is correct. Don't worry, the heat destroys the pungency of the mustard, leaving behind a mild, nutty flavour. The mustard also enhances the flavour of the other ingredients.

700 g (1½ lb) lean pork
1 tablespoon of mustard powder
50 g (2 oz) margarine
2 onions, sliced
900 ml (1½ pt) chicken stock
Good pinch mixed herbs
Salt and freshly ground black pepper
1 medium cooking apple, peeled and grated
1 tablespoon cornflour
Heaped teaspoon chopped fresh parsley

Cooking time: In a saucepan — about 1 hour
In the oven — about 1¾ hours **(180°C — 350°F — Gas 4)**

Cut the pork into bite size pieces and toss them in the mustard powder. Then fry them in the margarine until browned all over. Transfer to a saucepan or casserole. Fry the onions until soft and add to the meat. Pour in the stock and add mixed herbs, salt, pepper, and the grated apple. Bring saucepan to the boil, put lid on and simmer until meat is tender. If using casserole, cover with lid and cook in the oven until meat is tender.

About 20 minutes before the end of the cooking time, blend the cornflour with a little cold water. Add to saucepan or casserole and stir. Continue with the cooking. This will thicken the juices nicely. Serve sprinkled with the chopped parsley.

Pork Parcels

Parcels were originally made of parchment, however nowadays foil is used. A see-through roasting bag makes a quick family size parcel.

For each serving allow:
1 lean pork chop
15 g (about ½ oz) margarine
Dessertspoon of finely chopped onion

25 g (1 oz) mushrooms, thinly sliced

Salt and freshly ground black pepper

Pinch mixed herbs

1 – 2 tablespoons cream or milk

Cooking time: About 40 minutes **(190°C — 375°F — Gas 5)**

Fry the chops in the margarine to brown well on each side and place side by side in a tin or oven-proof dish. Lightly fry the onion and mushrooms and spoon over the chops. Season with salt, pepper and a tiny pinch of mixed herbs per chop. Finally, spoon the cream on top.

Roasting Bag Parcel:
Place the whole tin or oven-proof dish into the roasting bag. Suck out the air and close the bag very near the opening, this allows plenty of space inside the bag for steam. There must be no holes in the bag.

Bake until chops are tender. Do not open bag until cooking has finished, (the bag will balloon right up during cooking). Serve chops with the lovely juices.

To make foil parcels (individual or family size)

The nice thing about individual parcels is that they are served unopened so that the diner enjoys the wonderful aroma that escapes when the parcel is first opened. Foil baked chops have a nice creamy colour. The foil must be large enough to fold over and cover the chop or chops. The edges must be sealed together with a double fold yet the parcel must be loose fitting to allow room for the steam inside to expand. There must be no hole in the foil. Place parcels on a tin to bake. Cooking time is the same as with roasting bag parcel.

Breaded Pork Chops

Small chops can be made go further by coating them in breadcrumbs. Naturally, this dish is high in calories because the breadcrumbs soak up the fat, but the chops taste delicious.

Dip the pork chops in seasoned flour, then into beaten egg and finally into well flavoured breadcrumbs (see page 46).

Fry in plenty of margarine or oil until golden brown on each side. If all the chops fit on the pan, continue cooking them over a gentle heat until cooked through (about 25 minutes or so). If you have too many, transfer chops to a tin, loosely cover with foil and continue cooking in a hot oven **(200°C — 400°F — Gas 6)** for about 45 minutes. Serve with gravy and vegetables of your choice.

A breadcrumb coating is much tastier if you season the breadcrumbs with salt, pepper, good pinch of mixed herbs, finely chopped parsley and even a little very finely chopped onion.

Crunchy Lamb Squares *(Serves 4-6)*

Really economical and tasty, to boot! The first stage of preparation must be done a few hours in advance so it is not a "bung in the oven" recipe.

2 – 3 breasts of lamb, (as lean as you can get)
1 onion
1 carrot
1 stick celery
Salt and freshly ground black pepper
¼ teaspoon mixed herbs
Water
To coat:
A little flour
1 large egg, beaten
1 – 2 mugfuls breadcrumbs (nicely flavoured)
Fat for frying

Stage 1. Trim any pieces of excess fat off the breasts. Chop the vegetables and put into a saucepan with the meat. Season with salt, pepper and mixed herbs. Pour in enough cold water to cover the contents. Bring to the boil and simmer gently until the meat is tender (about 1½ hours). Lift out the breasts of lamb and flatten them between two boards or tins, (with something heavy on top). Leave to cool for a few hours.

Stage 2. When cold, cut the flattened breasts into squares or wide fingers. Dip each into the flour, then into beaten egg and finally into the breadcrumbs. Fry in margarine, lard or oil until a nice crisp golden brown and meat is heated through. Serve with gravy and vegetables.

Note: The liquid in the saucepan is perfect stock for a vegetable soup. Lift off the fat when it cools.

Pork Chops in a Tangy Orange Sauce *(Serves 4-6)*

Make a special meal of pork chops by cooking them until deliciously succulent in this tangy sauce.

4 – 6 lean pork chops
50 g (2 oz) margarine
1 large onion, thinly sliced
Juice 2 large oranges
400 – 570 ml (¾ – 1 pt) water
½ – 1 chicken stock cube
1 dessertspoon sugar
½ level teaspoon of ground ginger
6 cardamon seeds (optional)
Salt and freshly ground black pepper
2 – 3 tablespoons vinegar
1 rounded tablespoon cornflour
1 – 2 tablespoons cream
To serve: 1 orange, cut in slices
Chopped parsley

Fry the chops in the margarine until browned on each side. Arrange them in a single layer in a large saucepan. Fry the onions until soft and add to the chops. Add in all the other ingredients except the cornflour and cream. The chops should be just covered in the liquid. Put the lid on the saucepan, bring to the boil and then simmer very gently until the chops are nicely tender. This will take a good 50 minutes. Transfer the chops to a serving dish. Blend the cornflour with cold water and add to the saucepan juices. Bring to the boil, stirring all the time. Simmer for 2 – 3 minutes then pour over the chops. Sprinkle chopped parsley on top and decorate with slices of orange.

Roast Lamb with Garlic

Give your roast lamb a touch of class!

Joint of lamb for roasting. (Fillet or shank or shoulder. Allow about 175 g (6 oz) meat without bone per serving, or 225 g (8 oz) with bone)
2 cloves garlic, chopped

Grated rind 1 lemon

Rosemary, fresh or dried

Salt and freshly ground black pepper

Cooking time: Allow 20 minutes cooking time for every 450 g (1 lb) of meat. Then allow an extra 20 minutes at the end.
(190°C — 375°F — Gas 5)

Place the meat in a roasting tin. Sprinkle the garlic, lemon rind and rosemary over the lamb and season with salt and pepper. Cover loosely with foil and roast in the oven. Baste meat occasionally with the juices in the pan. Remove foil for last half hour. Allow meat to "rest" near the cooker for 15 minutes after roasting, before carving, as this makes the job easier.

Remove fat from the roasting juices and add to the gravy.

Note: For extra flavour: Before roasting, brown the joint of lamb all over in melted margarine in a frying pan. Then continue as above.

To remove fat from any roasting juices: Put juices in a narrow container so the top surface is not too wide. Drop in a few cubes of ice and these will set the fat quickly so that it can be easily removed.

Special Kidney Gravy

This is so delicious it nearly makes a meal in itself. It gives great "body" to any lamb dish, and it makes small chops seem much bigger!

1 lamb kidney

25 g (1 oz) margarine

1 small onion, chopped

1 clove garlic, chopped

6 — 8 mushrooms, chopped

Salt and freshly ground black pepper

1 rounded teaspoon *each* of gravy powder and a brown soup powder

400 ml (¾ pt) water

The fat free juices from the roast (if available)

Remove fat from the kidney if necessary. Chop kidney, discarding the core (the white bits in the centre).

Fry the onion and garlic in the margarine until soft. Add in the kidney pieces and mushrooms and fry until kidney is cooked (over cooking toughens kidneys). Season with salt and pepper. Blend the gravy and soup powder with the water and add to the kidneys. Then add the roasting juices. Bring to the boil and serve.

Slices of cold roast lamb are delicious if reheated in this gravy.

Note: This gravy is tasty even without the kidney.

Lasagne *(Serves 8) posh nosh!*

The Italians can be justifiably proud of their lasagne. It looks good, it tastes good and it freezes well. Served with a salad and crusty bread, it makes a delicious meal.

Step 1. THE MEAT SAUCE
Don't be put off by the long list of ingredients, none of them are unusual but each adds a little touch to the flavour.

1 onion, finely chopped
2 cloves garlic chopped
50 g (2 oz) margarine
4 streaky rashers (optional)
450 g (1 lb) minced beef
25g (1 oz) flour
1 tin tomatoes
275 ml (½ pt) stock (or water and stock cube)
2 tablespoons tomato purée
Salt and freshly ground black pepper
Bay leaf
½ teaspoon oregano
Thin strips of lemon peel (no white pith)
Generous pinches of ground nutmeg
1 carrot, finely chopped
1 celery stick, chopped

Fry the onion and garlic in the margarine until soft. Then add in the rashers (chopped) and fry for a couple of minutes. Next add in the meat. Fry thoroughly until nicely browned all over.

If your pan is not large enough, use a heavy, big saucepan.

Remove excess fat after frying (tilt pan to allow it run down). Leave 1 table-spoon of fat behind. Mix the flour through the meat mixture. Then pour in the tin of tomatoes and the stock and bring to the boil. As it is coming to the boil, add in all the remaining ingredients. Cover the pan and simmer for about 15 minutes. The mixture should be thickish, not runny. If it is runny, simmer with the lid off until it reaches the right consistency.

Step 2. THE CHEESE SAUCE

I love several layers of cheese sauce through the lasagne and so the ingredients for this sauce are generous! I find a very mild cheese sauce is best.

110 g (4 oz) margarine or butter
110 g (4 oz) flour
1.1 litres (2 pt) milk
1 heaped teaspoon mustard
Salt and freshly ground black pepper
50 g (2 oz) grated cheese

Put all the ingredients except the cheese into a large saucepan. Bring to the boil, stirring briskly with a whisk. Once the mixture becomes smooth, change to a wooden spoon. After boiling, add the cheese. Simmer for 2—3 minutes.

Note: If preferred, cheese sauce can be made using the traditional method as on page 67.

Step 3. THE LASAGNE

Use about 16—18 sheets of lasagne — enough for 3 layers. No preparation is required. You can choose between the straightforward lasagne, the green spinach lasagne or the whole wheat lasagne.

Step 4. TO ASSEMBLE

Use a rectangular dish (about 30.5 cm × 23 cm/12″ × 9″). Spread ¼ of the cheese sauce in a layer over the base and arrange a layer of lasagne on top. Spoon half the meat sauce over this and cover with more cheese sauce (another ¼). The second layer of lasagne is now put in place. Cover with remaining meat sauce. On top of this, spread another ¼ of cheese sauce. The last layer of lasagne is arranged next and then the final layer of cheese sauce goes on top.

Step 5. THE COOKING
Cooking time: 45-60 minutes **(190°C — 375°F — Gas 5).** Place in the upper half of the oven and cook until golden brown all over and lightly bubbling! Twenty minutes before the end, sprinkle a handful of grated cheese over the top.

Note: To prepare in advance, complete steps 1—4. Cover and store in the fridge for 2—3 days. Take out of the fridge about 2 hours before baking. Lasagne will keep up to three months in the freezer. This big lasagne will take at least 12 hours to thaw.

Country Pie *(Serves 6-8)*

A real family favourite. The crunchy wholemeal pastry contrasts nicely with the meat sauce. Half the ingredients makes 4 servings.

Wholemeal shortcrust pastry using 400 g (14 oz) flour, (page 78) or packet frozen puff pastry (350 g/12 oz).
Meat sauce:
1 medium onion, chopped
1—2 cloves garlic, chopped
25 g (1 oz) margarine
450 g (1 lb) minced beef
Salt and freshly ground black pepper
1 heaped teaspoon *each* of gravy powder and a beef soup powder
400 ml (¾ pt) water
¼ teaspoon mixed herbs
A few pinches ground nutmeg
110 g (4 oz) frozen mixed vegetables (optional)

Tin: Small Swiss roll tin 28 cm × 18 cm (11″ × 7″) greased. Use half the recipe and bake in a sandwich tin (20.5 cm/8″ in diameter).

Cooking time: 40—45 minutes **(200°C — 400°F — Gas 6)** (35 minutes smaller tin).

Fry the onion and garlic in the margarine until soft. Add the minced beef and fry until well browned. This takes a little time but adds greatly to the flavour. Season with salt and pepper. Tilt the pan to let the excess fat run down and spoon it out. Add the gravy and soup powders and the water to the pan. Bring to the boil (stirring). Flavour with mixed herbs and nutmeg. The sauce should be neither too thick nor too runny. (If too runny simmer gently to allow some of the liquid evaporate.) Add in the vegetables (thawed).

Roll out half the pastry and line the tin. Pour in the filling. Cover with remaining pastry. Wet edges and press together. Pierce a few holes in the top.

Bake in the upper half of the oven until pastry is well cooked.

Apple 'n Beef Balls *(Serves 5-6)*

You don't actually taste the apple but it does seem to "lighten" the flavour of this dish.

1 medium onion, finely chopped
1–2 cloves garlic, finely chopped (optional)
25 g (1 oz) margarine
450 g (1 lb) minced beef
1 medium cooking apple, peeled
50 g (2 oz) porridgemeal (rolled oats)
Salt and freshly ground black pepper
Generous pinches of ground nutmeg
¼ teaspoon mixed herbs
1 large egg
1 packet tomato soup (or beef)
Generous 570 ml (1 pt) water

Cooking time: 45—50 minutes **(200°C — 400°F — Gas 6)**

Fry the onion and garlic in the margarine until golden and add to the minced meat in a bowl. Grate the apple into the bowl and then add in all the remaining ingredients except the soup and the water. Mix very thoroughly. Shape into balls, about the size of golf balls. Place them side by side, not touching, in an ovenproof dish, (avoid a dish that is too wide, or the soup when added, will be too shallow).

Put the meatballs in the oven, for about 10—15 minutes to "set" and slightly brown. Meanwhile make up the packet of soup with the water in usual way. Take meat balls out of the oven and spoon off any excess fat that may have oozed out. Pour in the soup. Cover dish with foil and return to oven. Cook for a further 25—30 minutes.

Serve these succulent meatballs with the lovely soupy juices.

Italian Meat Puffs *(Serves 4-5)*

This recipe is like the miracle of the loaves and the fishes — it makes a little meat go a long way! My family love these as a snack or as a meal with vegetables.

1 small onion, chopped
15 g (about ½ oz) margarine
275 g (10 oz) minced beef
1 packet of Bolognese sauce
200 ml (not quite ½ pt) water
350 g (12 oz) frozen puff pastry

Cooking time: 15—20 minutes **(200°C — 400°F — Gas 6)**

Fry the onion in the margarine until soft. Add in the meat and fry until well browned. Spoon off excess fat. Mix the packet of sauce with the water and add to the meat. Bring to the boil and then cook gently until the mixture is mushy and not runny.

Roll out the pastry into a big square, 51 cm × 51 cm (20″ × 20″). Divide the square evenly into quarters. Divide each of these evenly in quarters again. Now you will have sixteen squares of pastry, 12.5 cm × 12.5 cm (5″ × 5″). Put a spoonful of meat mixture on a square, wet the edges of the pastry with water. Fold one corner of the square right over to the opposite corner — so the square becomes a triangle! Press the edges well to seal together. Place on greased baking tray. Repeat with all the squares. Bake in the oven. They will puff up nicely and turn a lovely golden brown.

Next time use a packet of curry sauce and call them Indian Meat Parcels!

Boboutie *(Serves 4-6)*

This minced beef dish is flavoured with curry powder and chutney and then baked.

2 eggs

2 slices of bread (preferably wholemeal)

150 ml (¼ pt) milk

2 medium onions, chopped

1 – 2 cloves of garlic (optional)

25 g (1 oz) margarine

450 g (1 lb) minced beef

2 level dessertspoons curry powder (or paste)

Salt and freshly ground black pepper

Pinch mixed herbs

2 dessertspoons chutney (preferably mango)

25 – 50 g (1 – 2 oz) blanched almonds (optional but nice)

Cooking time: 45 minutes **(180°C – 350°F – Gas 4)**

Beat the eggs together in a bowl. Break up or crumb the bread and add to the eggs with the milk. Leave to soak. Fry the onions and garlic in the margarine until soft then add in the minced beef. Fry until well browned. Tilt pan to allow excess fat drain down. Spoon it off. Add the curry to the meat along with the salt, pepper, mixed herbs and chutney. Stir the egg mixture into the meat to make a nice loose mixture, (not runny). Pour into a greased ovenproof dish, sprinkle the almonds on top. Bake in upper half of oven until set and nicely browned. Serve with the vegetables of your choice.

VEGETABLES

The fresher the vegetables, the better!

Once a vegetable or fruit is picked, its vitamin C content begins to diminish. If it is cut or chopped, the destruction of the vitamin C is speeded up. So, ideally prepare vegetables and salads as near to being eaten as is convenient. Vegetables and fruit provide our daily diet with low calorie bulk as well as important vitamins and minerals. A head of cauliflower has about the same number of calories as 25 g (1 oz) of butter or margarine. But try spreading a cauliflower on your bread!

Steaming vegetables is a good way to conserve their nutritional content. I have a little mini-steamer that has "petals" round the edge, which move to fit any size of saucepan. I find it of great use. The microwave is an excellent way to cook vegetables too.

Bavarian Style Cabbage *(Serves 4-6)*

Choose green, red or white cabbage. The extra ingredients make this a very tasty dish. If you increase the number of rashers, it can be served as a main dish accompanied by potatoes.

¼ – ½ head of cabbage 450 – 700 g (1 – 1½ lb)
2 – 4 rashers
50 g (2 oz) margarine
½ medium onion, chopped
1 – 2 cloves garlic, chopped
150 ml (¼ pt) stock (chicken or beef)
1 – 2 tablespoons mango chutney (see note)
1 bay leaf
¼ teaspoon of caraway seeds
Salt and freshly ground black pepper

Shred the cabbage finely, discarding the thickest stalks. Chop the rashers and fry in the margarine (in a heavy saucepan) until golden. Lift out. Next fry the onion and garlic until soft. Put the cabbage into the saucepan, stir, add back the rashers plus all the remaining ingredients. Cover with lid and cook gently until just tender. Serve.

Note: If you have no chutney, use 1-2 teaspoons of lemon juice or vinegar and 1 teaspoon of sugar.

Cabbage – "plain honest to goodness"

Cabbage is one of the most maligned vegetables. The mere mention of it makes many children run for cover! To conserve its nutritional value and flavour shred it very finely (in food processor if available) and cook in the minimum amount of **water or stock** (about 1 cm/½″ deep) in a strong wide saucepan, so the cabbage is in a shallow layer. Keep lid on while cooking. Whatever bit of liquid is left in the pot, when the cabbage is *just* tender, can be added to a gravy or soup. Season with **salt and freshly ground black pepper**. Check occasionally as it cooks to ensure water doesn't evaporate, causing the cabbage to burn.

Creamed Cabbage

Serve the **cooked cabbage** covered with a **White** or **Parsley Sauce** (page 67), add the litle bit of cooking juices to the sauce.

Spinach

Another of my favourite vegetables! Cut off the stalks and wash **450 g (1 lb) of fresh spinach** in lots of cold water. Put it dripping with water, into a saucepan. No more water is needed. Season with **salt and freshly ground black pepper**. Cover and cook gently for about 5—10 minutes, shaking occasionally. The bulk of the spinach reduces drastically on cooking. Strain off any liquid (use in a soup). Slice through the spinach to make it easy to serve. Sprinkle with **ground nutmeg** which gives it a delicious flavour. For an occasional treat stir some **fresh cream** through the cooked spinach.

Skinny Spinach!

Cooked spinach topped with **Thick Cheese Dressing** (page 64) makes a great low calorie snack meal for weight watchers.

Colcannon *(Serves 4)*

This is a traditional Irish dish for Hallowe'en — that day of the year when the "little people" move from their summer quarters to their winter quarters! Kale is the correct vegetable to use but cabbage will do, treat it in the same way as Kale. A little mace gives a lovely flavour to the finished dish.

Generous 700 g (1½ lb) potatoes
225 g (8 oz) Kale (6 — 8 leaves) or 225 g (8 oz cabbage)
1 onion, sliced
150 ml (¼ pt) milk
Salt and freshly ground black pepper
¼ teaspoon ground mace
50 g (2 oz) butter (optional)

Steam or boil the peeled potatoes until tender. Meanwhile prepare the kale — wash it thoroughly. Cut out and discard the big stalk that runs up the centre of each leaf. Shred leaves finely and cook in minimum amount of water (about 2.5 cm/1″ deep) with lid on, over a gentle heat, until tender. Check occasionally to ensure water does not evaporate before kale is tender. Prepare the onion by cooking it in the milk until soft. Mash the potatoes and mix in the kale, milk and onion. Season with salt and pepper and flavour with mace. Pile into a hot dish. Place the butter in a hole in the top and it will melt deliciously.

Potatoes in Milk *(Serves 2-4)*

Surprisingly, this is an Italian recipe. It is very convenient if you're in a hurry. Simply wash and scrape **1 medium potato per person**. Slice very thinly. (Don't wash after slicing as this will remove the starch that is necessary to thicken the milk.) Put into a wide, heavy saucepan. Pour in about 1 cm (½″) deep of **milk**, (use **slimline** if you wish). Season with **salt and freshly ground black pepper.** Put lid on, bring to boil and then simmer very gently until potatoes are tender. Check frequently to see they don't burn. Serve sprinkled with a **pinch of ground nutmeg**. It is not suitable for a large number of potatoes as the milk will burn before they are tender.

Heaven and Earth

This is a simplified version of a German recipe. All you do is add a few tablespoons of **sweetened stewed apple** (heaven) to your **mashed potatoes** (earth). It gives them a lovely sharp, sweet taste.

Roast Potatoes

Roast potatoes are much crisper if cooked in a separate tin from the roast. They will roast more quickly if first boiled for 5 minutes. Put the peeled **potatoes** into a saucepan of cold water and bring to the boil. Simmer gently for 5 minutes and then drain. Melt a piece of **margarine or lard** in a tin, put in the potatoes and brush all over with the fat. Roast for approximately 1 hour in a hot oven **(200°C — 400°F — Gas 6)**. If the meat is cooking at a lower temperature allow a little longer time. If necessary, raise the oven heat at the end to brown. During cooking, baste potatoes with some of the tasty fat from the meat.

Note: The 5 minutes boiling is not essential. If omitted, roast the potatoes for about 2 hours.

Milky Bake Potatoes

Wash and scrape **one medium potato per person**. Slice very thinly, keeping slices in place and sit into greased ovenproof dish. Press out the potatoes so that the slices fan out in neat overlapping lines. Pour in enough **milk or cream** (depending on your hip measurements!) to half cover the slices. Season with **salt and freshly ground black pepper**. Loosely cover with a piece of foil. Bake for about 50 — 60 minutes at **190°C — 375°F — Gas 5**. Remove foil after 30 minutes. Sprinkle with **ground nutmeg** before serving.

Note: Ideal for microwave cooking — use a deep dish as the milk boils over. Cook on high for about 10 minutes.

> Potatoes are a good food! The most nutritious part of potatoes is just under the skin, so avoid peeling whenever possible.

Ratatouille *(Serves 5-6) posh nosh!*

One day, when cooking a saucepan of ratatouille beside a saucepan of rhubarb, I added the sugar to the wrong one. Despite frantic spooning it was impossible to remove all the sugar. The resulting ratatouille was lovely. Ever since, I include sugar in the ingredients! (In fact, a little sugar enhances many vegetable dishes). Ratatouille with its wonderful Mediterranean colours makes any meal special. It can be eaten hot or cold.

1 large onion 275 g (10 oz)

2 — 4 cloves garlic, finely chopped

6 — 10 tablespoons oil (preferably olive)

1 aubergine 275 g (10 oz)

2 small courgettes 275 g (10 oz)

1 small red pepper 175 g (6 oz)	
5 large tomatoes 550 g (1¼ lbs)	
Salt and freshly ground black pepper	
¼ teaspoon oregano	
1 dessertspoon sugar	

For the best flavour, fry each vegetable on its own and then put them together in a large saucepan. I use two frying pans to speed up the job! First chop each vegetable into bite size chunks, but don't chop the aubergine until you are ready to fry it as it discolours quickly. When chopping the courgette and the aubergine, ensure that there is a piece of skin on each bit. Start by frying the onions and garlic until soft and golden. Transfer them to the saucepan, leaving as much of the oil behind as possible. Then fry the aubergine and allow the pieces to brown slightly. Transfer to the saucepan. There is no need to brown any of the other vegetables, just fry them for a few minutes to flavour them. When all the vegetables have been put into the saucepan, season well with salt and pepper and flavour with oregano and sugar. Cook gently with the lid on for about 15—30 minutes. A few chopped fresh basil leaves — if you can get them — is the proper herb to stir through, before serving.

Calorie Conscious Ratatouille

Whilst not exactly the same, this low oil way of cooking ratatouille is a very good copy of the original. Use the above recipe with **only 2 tablespoons of oil,** in which you fry the onion and garlic until just golden. Then put all the chopped vegetables in a large saucepan with barely **150 ml (¼ pt) of chicken stock.** Cook gently (lid on) until tender, stirring occasionally.

Ratatouille reheats very well. It is also suitable for freezing (up to two months).

Mustardy Cauliflower *(Serves 4-6)*

This is one of my favourite ways to serve cauliflower. The florets are cooked in milk which is then used to make the sauce — none of the goodness is lost.

1 head cauliflower
275 ml (½ pt) milk
Salt and freshly ground black pepper
25 g (1 oz) *each* flour and margarine
teaspoon mustard, a nice grainy one

Divide cauliflower into florets and cut a cross deeply into the stalk of each one, (this speeds up cooking time). Arrange in a single layer in a saucepan, pour in milk and season with salt and pepper. Bring to the boil, then simmer gently with lid on — until just tender. It is a help to turn over the florets half way through the cooking. Arrange florets in a vegetable dish. Use a fork to mash together the flour and the margarine. Drop this paste in little pieces into the milk and stir briskly with a whisk while bringing to the boil. Add the mustard and season if necessary. Simmer for 2—3 minutes and pour over cauliflower.

Variations: Add 50g (2 oz) grated cheese to the sauce with the mustard or, omit mustard and add 1 tablespoon chopped parsley instead.

Marrowfat Peas (Serves 4-6)

It is amazing what one will do for love! "Himself" loves marrowfat peas and I didn't. It was the skins floating in a layer on top of the cooking water that really drove me wild. Then I discovered that if I only add enough water to barely cover the peas the skins simply cannot float off!

1 packet of marrowfat peas
¼ of stock cube
Slice of onion
Generous pinch mixed herbs
Salt and freshly ground black pepper

Steep peas overnight covered in water, (use only 1 of the soda discs). Drain and rinse. Place in a saucepan, only barely cover with water and add in the other ingredients. Bring to the boil and simmer very gently until just tender (with lid on), takes about 25 minutes. Remove lid and simmer very gently to evaporate most of the water and make peas a bit mushy. Be careful not to let them burn!

Note: If you have a tasty soup or stew to hand, add a ladleful to the cooking water instead of the stock cube.

Parsnip and Apple
Peel and chop **1—2 parsnips** and place in a steamer along with ½ **cooking apple** (peeled and chopped). Season with **salt and freshly ground black pepper**. Cook until tender, then mash together. This gives a lovely sharp, sweet flavour to the parsnips.

Speckled Swedes

Peel and slice **one swede turnip**. Cook until tender in boiling salted water, flavoured with a **piece of stock cube**. Drain and mash (or "buzz" in food processor) together with a **tablespoon of chopped parsley**. The flecks of green parsley look very attractive through the golden coloured purée.

Braised Celery with Orange Juice *(Serves 4-6)*

The orange juice gives a lovely fresh taste to the juices of this dish. It can be reheated easily and it is low in calories.

½ – 1 head of celery
275 ml (½ pt) water
1 vegetable stock cube
Salt and freshly ground black pepper
Teaspoon grated orange rind
2 rounded teaspoons cornflour
Juice of 1 orange

Top, tail and wash the celery sticks. Cut into short, even lengths (wide stalks can be split in two). Put them into a saucepan with the water, stock cube, salt, pepper and grated orange rind. Bring to the boil, cover with lid and simmer gently until celery is just tender. Transfer the celery to a hot dish. Blend the cornflour with the orange juice and stir into the liquid in the saucepan. Bring to the boil to thicken. Simmer for 2—3 minutes and pour over celery.

Celery and Cashew Stir Fry *(Serves 4-6)*

This nice crunchy vegetable dish is good with chicken, turkey or pork dishes.

½ – 1 head celery
50 g – 110 g (2 – 4 oz) cashew nuts
1 – 2 tablespoons of oil
Salt and freshly ground black pepper

Top and tail the celery sticks. Wash and slice very thinly. Steam or boil them (for about 5 minutes) until just tender. Drain. Shortly before serving, fry the cashew nuts (for about 5 minutes) in the oil until golden and add in the celery pieces. Toss them together over the heat for a few minutes. Season with salt and pepper.

Sprouts in Parsley Sauce *(Serves 4-6)*

If you find the flavour of sprouts a bit strong, try serving them coated with parsley sauce as this mellows them nicely. Before steaming or boiling the sprouts cut a cross into the stalk end of each one as this speeds up the cooking. Be careful not to overcook. Parsley sauce recipe is on page 67.

Sprout Purée *(Serves 4-6)*

This is delightful. Simply mash or "buzz" together 450 g (1 lb) cooked sprouts with 150 ml (¼ pt) parsley sauce. Season and flavour with generous pinches of ground nutmeg.

Lemon Baked Tomatoes *(Serves 4-6)*

It is an understatement to say I am partial to tomatoes. They are wonderfully convenient and low in calories.

4 – 6 tomatoes
1 – 2 bay leaves, cut in pieces
1 small onion
1 – 2 cloves garlic
1 tablespoon oil
Grated rind ½ lemon
Pinch mixed herbs
A little chopped parsley or basil

Skin the tomatoes (optional), cut in half. Lightly grease an ovenproof dish, scatter the bay leaf pieces in it and place the tomatoes (cut side up) on top. Finely chop the onion and garlic and fry in the oil until soft. Add the lemon rind and the mixed herbs and spoon this mixture over the tomatoes. Bake in the oven **(190°C – 375°F – Gas 5)** for about 15–25 minutes. Sprinkle with chopped parsley or basil and serve hot.

Salads

Nutritional experts advise us to eat about one third of our daily intake of vegetables and fruit in raw form. The combination of flavours and colours in a salad allows us display the 'artistic' side of our cooking talent! Ideally, salads should be eaten soon after preparation. If they have to be made in advance, don't add any onion until close to serving as it changes flavour.

Lightly toasted sunflower seeds or sesame seeds or pine kernels are delightful sprinkled on different salads. Spread seeds out under a medium grill to toast them.

Dressings

Don't drown salads in dressings! Mayonnaise and salad cream are popular basic dressings.

Low Calorie Dressing

Natural yoghurt makes a good low calorie dressing. I like to flavour it with a spoon of mustard or salad cream, salt and freshly ground black pepper.

Honey Dressing

1 dessertspoon *each* of honey and oil

1 desertspoon vinegar or lemon juice

Salt and freshly ground black pepper

Small spoon mustard

Mix all these together to make a lovely slightly sweet dressing.

Thick Cheese Dressing

This is really substantial! It really makes a meal of a salad. It is very low in calories and I find it very useful as a dressing for many things.

225 g (8 oz) cottage cheese

150 ml (¼ pt) carton natural yoghurt

Salt and freshly ground black pepper

Teaspoon mustard

"Buzz" all the ingredients together in a food processor, **or** press cottage cheese through a sieve and mix with the other ingredients. This will keep (covered) in the fridge for about a week.

Fruity Coleslaw *(Serves 4-6)*

Fruity coleslaw makes a delightful change from the inevitable carrot and cabbage combination. Green is my first choice of cabbage, though white or red are also suitable.

¼ – ½ head of cabbage
1 medium onion
1 apple, unpeeled
1 orange, cut in juicy segments (page 4)
50 – 110 g (2 – 4 oz) black grapes
1 – 2 dessertspoons freshly chopped parsley
Salt and freshly ground black pepper
2 – 3 tablespoons dressing (page 64)

Wash cabbage, drain and shred very finely. (A food processor is ideal for the job.) Put into a salad bowl. Chop the onion and apple. Cut the grapes in half and remove the pips. Put everything into the salad bowl and toss together.

Cooked chicken or turkey cut into chunks are very nice mixed through the coleslaw. Serve as a meal with crusty bread.

Cauliflower and Pepper Salad *(Serves 6)*

This salad breaks up a head of cauliflower into such small pieces it almost looks like rice!

1 small crisp head cauliflower
1 small red pepper
1 small green pepper
1 apple, unpeeled
Salt and freshly ground black pepper
Honey dressing (page 64)

Cut the cauliflower into florets and divide each one into its smaller florets. Now break or cut these into their tiniest florets. De-seed the peppers and chop them and the apple into very small pieces. Mix all the ingredients together in a salad bowl.

Crunchy Winter Salad *(Serves 4)*

Raw Brussels sprouts, thinly sliced, make an excellent base for a salad.

110 g (4 oz) Brussels sprouts
110 g (4 oz) cauliflower
1 medium carrot
1 small leek (or onion)
50 g (2 oz) sultanas
25 g (1 oz) toasted sunflower seeds
2 tablespoons dressing of your choice
Salt and freshly ground black pepper

Slice the Brussels sprouts very thinly, discarding the stalks. Cut the cauliflower into small florets. Cut the carrot into thin matchstick pieces. Slice the leek (or onion) very thinly. Mix everything together in a salad bowl.

Green Salad

A classic! Crisp lettuce is the base into which you add a variety of green vegetables or fruits. The following are the ingredients I use — not all at one time — but whatever I have handy on the day.

Lettuce, in small pieces or shredded
Iceberg lettuce, sliced
Chinese leaves, shredded
Brussels sprouts, chopped
Apple, chopped
Melon, chopped
Green grapes, halved
Kiwi, sliced and peeled
Green pepper, thinly sliced

Green beans or mangetout, cooked
Onion rings, thin
Leeks, thinly sliced
Avocado, chopped (added at the last minute)
Parsley, chopped
Salt and freshly ground black pepper
Dressing

Put your choice of vegetables and fruit into a salad bowl with salt, pepper and dressing. Toss everything together.

Basic White Sauce

This provides the base for many different sauces.

25 g (1 oz) margarine
25 g (1 oz) flour
275 ml (½ pt) milk
Salt and freshly ground black pepper

Traditional method:
Melt the margarine in a saucepan and stir in the flour. Allow to cook for a minute or two without browning. Stir constantly. Draw off heat and gradually stir in the liquid to make a smooth mixture (**or** add in all the milk and whisk briskly to mix well in a much shorter time). Add salt and pepper. Bring sauce to boil stirring continuously and then simmer for 2-3 minutes to ensure flour is cooked.

New method:
Put all the ingredients into a saucepan. Bring to the boil stirring briskly with a whisk. Once mixture is nice and smooth stir with a wooden spoon. Simmer for 2-3 minutes.

Parsley Sauce

I will eat old boots — providing they are covered with parsley sauce!

Put about **2 tablespoons of chopped fresh parsley** and a **lump of raw onion** into the **basic white sauce** after boiling. Simmer for 2-3 minutes and discard onion before serving.

To prevent a skin forming on a sauce — if it has to be kept standing — put a piece of wet greaseproof paper or a piece of foil right down onto the surface.

Vegetable Sauce For Pasta *(Serves 4-6)*

A lovely sauce to serve with pasta which makes a refreshing change.

1 carrot
1 onion
2 cloves garlic (optional)
1 small courgette
75 g (3 oz) mushrooms
1 stalk celery
A few florets cauliflower
75 g (3 oz) green beans
2 tomatoes
2 – 3 tablespoons oil or butter
½ pint chicken stock
Salt and freshly ground black pepper
1 tablespoon cornflour
1 tablespoon chopped fresh parsley
75 ml (3 oz) cream
Pinch ground nutmeg or mace

Prepare all the vegetables and cut into neat small pieces. Heat the oil or butter in a good wide saucepan and fry the vegetables gently without browning for 3-5 minutes. Add in stock, and season with the salt and pepper. Cover with a lid, bring to the boil and simmer gently until vegetables are just tender. Blend cornflour with a little water add to the sauce and bring to the boil. Then add in the parsley cream and nutmeg. Heat gently and serve on cooked spaghetti.

DESSERTS

Don't eat sugar...watch those calories...eat healthier foods... our ears ring with advice. It is true, though that like a constant drip of water, the food we eat on a day to day basis is what affects us for better or worse. The occasional self-indulgence is not the problem!

This section includes some of my favourite desserts. I also like to take full advantage of the great variety of fresh fruit available to treat my family to "instant" desserts.

Apricot and Almond Flan

This is particularly handy when there are few fresh fruits in season.

Sweet shortcrust pastry using 175 g (6 oz) flour (page 78)

Filling:

1 spoon apricot jam

1 tin apricot halves, drained

50 g (2 oz) margarine

50 g (2 oz) caster sugar

1 egg

½ teaspoon almond essence

1 egg white, beaten until stiff

50 g (2 oz) ground almonds

25 g (1 oz) flaked almonds (optional)

Tin: 21.5 cm (8½″) sandwich tin, greased.

Cooking time: About 45 minutes **(200°C — 400°F — Gas 6)**

Line the sandwich tin with the pastry. Spread the jam over the base and arrange the apricots in a layer on top (cut side down). Beat the margarine and sugar together until soft, then beat in the whole egg, almond essence and the ground almonds. The mixture will look a bit rough but don't worry! Finally, stir in the beaten egg white and spoon the mixture over the apricots. Sprinkle the flaked almonds over the top. (Nice for posh!) Bake on 2nd shelf until cooked and a good golden colour. If necessary, reduce the oven heat after 30 minutes cooking to **(180°C — 350°F — Gas 4)**.

Serve warm or cold with cream or thickened apricot juice. (Thicken juice with heaped teaspoon of cornflour blended with water. Bring to the boil and flavour with almond essence or lemon juice.)

Rhubarb Custard Pie *(Serves 5-6)*

A real family favourite. Even if you are not head over heels in love with rhubarb, you will enjoy this. Chopped rhubarb is placed in a pastry case topped with egg and milk and baked. Gooseberries can be used instead.

Sweet shortcrust pastry using 175 g (6 oz) flour (page 78).

Filling:

1 large bunch rhubarb

2 eggs

110 g (4 oz) sugar

Generous 150 ml (¼ pt) milk or cream

Tin: Sandwich tin or flan dish 23 cm (9″) diameter, greased.

Cooking time: about 40 minutes **(200°C — 400°F — Gas 6)**.

Line the sandwich tin with the rolled out pastry. Top, tail and wipe the rhubarb sticks. Cut into very thin slices about 1 cm (½″) long. Arrange in the pastry case, in a single layer. Beat the eggs, sugar and milk together and pour over the rhubarb. The liquid should just barely cover the rhubarb. Bake in the upper half of the oven until the filling is set and the top golden brown. If necessary, reduce the oven heat to **(180°C — 350°F — Gas 4)** after about 25—30 minutes. Serve hot or cold.

> The measurements I give for tins do not include the metal rim around the edge.

French Fruit Flan

The layer of cream cheese, flavoured with lemon juice, included in this fruit filled pastry case, gives it a lovely flavour. Redcurrant jelly (the kind you buy as jam) makes a lovely glaze. It is not always easy to get — so when you see it — buy it!

Sweet shortcrust pastry using 175 g (6 oz) flour (page 78).

Filling:

175 g (6 oz) cream cheese

25 g (1 oz) caster sugar

Juice ½ lemon
Fruit:
1−2 punnets strawberries
or **350 g (12 oz) black grapes (see note)**
Glaze:
2−3 tablespoons redcurrant jelly
or **1 small packet of quick setting jelly**

Tin: 23 cm (9″) sandwich tin, greased.

Cooking time: 15 minutes **(200°C − 400°F − Gas 6)**.

Roll out pastry, line tin and bake empty. (See page 79, for extra hints.) Allow to cool.

Beat the filling ingredients together until smooth and spread over pastry base, keeping a tablespoon to use for decoration. Prepare the fruit (cut strawberries in half, do likewise with grapes, removing the pips). Arrange the fruit in a layer over the filling. To glaze: soften the redcurrant jelly in a saucepan with a tablespoon of water. When it is a nice consistency, spoon over fruit. **Or** make up quick set jelly according to packet directions and spoon over fruit.

To decorate: Use an icing syringe and pipe the remaining cream cheese filling in tiny roses around the sides.

Note: Tinned peaches or other fruit of your choice are also suitable.

Strawberries

Having just mentioned strawberries — let me suggest you try **nice fresh strawberries** with a light dusting of **freshly ground black pepper** — no cream! Black pepper goes well on a lot of fresh fruit.

Strawberries with Orange

For a slightly sweeter tooth! Cut a **punnet of strawberries in quarters** and put in a bowl. Sprinkle the **juice of an orange** over them as well as a light dusting of **caster sugar**. Chill for about 1 hour before serving. The orange really enhances the flavour!

Brown Bread Ice Cream *(Serves 4-6)*

Wholemeal bread crumbs are baked in the oven with brown sugar until crisp. This gives a scrumptious crunch to the ice cream. The ginger adds an extra touch. This is very rich so serve in small portions. For special effect, serve in chocolate cups or fresh pear cups.

50 g (2 oz) wholemeal bread crumbs

50 g (2 oz) brown sugar

275 ml (½ pt) cream

1 tablespoon of caster sugar

A few drops of vanilla essence

Small teaspoon of grated fresh root ginger (optional)

Turn up fridge to its highest setting about 1 hour before starting unless you have a freezer.

Mix the breadcrumbs with the brown sugar and spread in a thin, even layer on a lightly oiled flat tin. Put into a hot oven **(200°C — 400°F — Gas 6)** until the sugar caramelises. You'll know when this has happened because the tin can be turned sideways and the crumbs won't move. It takes about 5 minutes or so. Don't let it burn! Remove "sheet" of crumbs from the tin and break up into fine crumbs again, using rolling pin or food processor.

Meanwhile, whip the cream with the vanilla and sugar until fairly thick. Put into ice box or freezer until half set.

When half set, take out and whip in the crumbs and the ginger. Return to icebox or freezer. When half set again, remove and whip once more. (This helps give a smoother ice cream.) Then freeze completely.

Place in the fridge about 1 hour before serving.

Fresh pear cups: Allow one per person. Peel the pear leaving the stalk intact. Cut a piece off the base so pear can stand upright. Cut the pear across (about ⅓ down from stalk). Scoop out a good bit of the centre. Just before serving, fill generously with the ice cream and put top back on.

Chocolate cups are available in shops.

Pineapple Cheesecake *(Serves 8) posh nosh!*

This is a lovely fresh-tasting cheesecake suitable for a special occasion.

Base:

225 g (8 oz) digestive biscuits

25 g (1 oz) caster sugar

110 g (4 oz) melted butter

Pinch ground nutmeg

Cheesecake:

1½ small packets of gelatine (20 g / ¾ oz)

375 g (13 oz) tin pineapple rings or chunks

225 g (8 oz) cottage cheese

225 g (8 oz) cream cheese

Juice small lemon

2 eggs, separated

110 g (4 oz) caster sugar

150 ml (¼ pt) cream

Tin: Use a round tin 23 cm (9″) diameter with a removable base, lightly oiled.

Dissolve the gelatine in the pineapple juice. Do this in a microwave or by standing the mug in a saucepan of simmering water. Allow to cool. Put the cottage cheese and cream cheese into a food processor (see note) and "buzz" until smooth. Add in lemon juice, egg yolks, sugar and pineapple, also the cooled gelatine and cream and "buzz" all together. Put into a bowl and chill in the fridge until mixture begins to thicken. Meanwhile make the base.

Biscuit base: Crush the biscuits finely (in a bag using a rolling pin). Add them to the melted butter with the sugar and nutmeg. Spread in an even layer in the base of the tin.

Stiffly whip the egg whites and fold them through the cheese mixture when it has stiffened (not set). Pour into prepared tin and chill for a few hours.

To serve: Lift the bottom out of the tin and place on a plate. Decorate the top with whipped cream "roses" or small pieces of pineapple.

Note: If a food processor is not available, sieve the cottage cheese and finely chop the pineapple and mix with the cream cheese, lemon juice, egg yolks, sugar, gelatine and cream.

Quick Pink Cheesecake

The juice of the fruit and the jelly give a nice pink colour to this cheesecake.

1 packet raspberry jelly

1 tin raspberries

225 g (8 oz) cottage cheese

225 g (8 oz) cream cheese

2 eggs, separated

25 g (1 oz) caster sugar

Biscuit base: As for the Pineapple Cheesecake.

Tin: Round tin 23 cm (9") diameter with a removable base, lightly oiled.

Dissolve the jelly in the juice of the raspberries. Put the cottage cheese, cream cheese, egg yolks and sugar into a food processor and "buzz" until smooth. If a food processor is not available, sieve the cottage cheese and then mix thoroughly with the cream cheese, egg yolks and sugar. Stir cheese mixture into the jelly and put it into the fridge to thicken (not set).

Meanwhile make the biscuit base — see Pineapple Cheesecake recipe (page 73).

Whisk the egg whites until very stiff and stir gently but thoroughly through the jelly mixture once it gets thick (not set). Pour into prepared tin and chill for 2—3 hours.

Serve slices of the cheesecake accompanied with spoonfuls of tinned raspberries.

Apple Strudel

A special occasion apple tart! The wafer thin noodle paste is easy to make — except it does require a little time to spread it out. So take the phone off the hook, shut the kitchen door and enjoy doing it!

Noodle paste:

1 dessertspoon oil

1 egg yolk

A little water

110 g (4 oz) flour (not self raising)

Oil (for brushing)

Filling:

3 large cooking apples
50−75 g (2−3 oz) sugar (white or brown)
25 g (1 oz) flour
50 g (2 oz) raisins or sultanas
Generous pinches of cinnamon
50 g (2 oz) walnuts, chopped
Grated rind of small orange

Tin: A large Swiss roll tin 35.5 cm × 23 cm (14″ × 9″). Use it upside down so that the strudel can slide off.

Cooking Time: 35−40 minutes **(220°C − 425°F − Gas 7)**. After 10 minutes reduce to **(190°C − 375°F − Gas 5)**.

Mix the oil into the egg yolk and add just enough water to make up 75 ml (⅛ pt). Add liquid to flour and make a dough. Turn out onto a lightly floured board and knead it like the "divil!" This toughens the flour. Put on a plate, cover with a bowl and leave to rest for 30 minutes.

Meanwhile prepare the filling. Peel and dice the apples very finely (to ensure quick cooking). Then mix all the filling ingredients together in a bowl.

Roll out the noodle paste into a smallish rectangle. Spread a clean teatowel out on the table and sprinkle it with flour. Place the rectangle of noodle paste in the centre. Brush the paste lightly with oil. Put your fingertips in under the noodle paste and gently tease it out, stretching it gradually. Work on a small area at one time, brushing lightly with oil when necessary to keep the paste supple. Eventually you will stretch the paste out to cover at least three quarters of the teatowel. It will be very thin. If you try to rush the job you will make a hole! (....a silent prayer in case you do!). At worst, patch a hole with a piece from the edge − after all the stretching has been finished.

Place the filling ingredients in a long pile down the centre of the noodle paste (with slightly more in the central area). Fold one side of the noodle paste over the filling, do this by lifting the teatowel underneath, not the paste itself, it is too thin. Brush along the edge with water and then lift up the other side in the same way. Press edges together. Gather in the excess paste at each end.

Put the prepared tin right alongside the strudel. Use the teatowel to lift strudel onto the tin, gently rolling it over so the join is underneath. If you can, shape the strudel into a half crescent shape at the same time. Once it sits on the tin, don't try to move it. Bake in the top half of a hot oven for 10 minutes to cook the paste. Then reduce the heat and bake until apples are tender. To test use a skewer through the top.

Slide gently off the tin onto a serving plate. Cool a little, sieve some icing sugar on top. Decorate with cherries and angelica. Serve with whipped cream. Flavour cream with a liqueur if you wish.

Fresh Fruit Salad *(Serves 5-6)*

A tin of strawberries makes a lovely juicy base for the salad into which you add as many different fruits as you wish — the more the merrier!

1 tin strawberries (*or* sugar syrup)
2 peaches, don't peel
2 bananas, peeled
1 red apple and 1 green, don't peel
2 oranges, (cut into juicy segments see page 4)
2 plums
175 g (6 oz) black grapes, cut in half
2 kiwis, peeled
Wedge of melon, peeled
1 pear, peeled

Remove any stones or pips and chop the fruit. Add to the strawberries (or sugar syrup) and chill.

To make **sugar syrup**: Dissolve **110 g (4 oz) of sugar** in **150 ml (¼ pt) water** or white wine. Then boil briskly for about 3—5 minutes. Add juice of a lemon and a little Kirsch (optional).

Apple Purée

Give a twist to stewed apples by cooking them with their skins on! Prepare by chopping the unpeeled cooking apples and discarding the cores. Stew in a little water until tender, sweeten with sugar and then press through a sieve to remove the skins. Flavour with a little ground nutmeg and serve reheated or cold. This has a lovely smooth taste.

Coconut and Oatmeal Topping

This is a great crunchy topping for stewed apples making them quite a substantial dessert.

50 g (2 oz) coconut
75 – 110 g (3 – 4 oz) margarine
50 g (2 oz) porridgemeal (rolled oats)
25 g (1 oz) caster sugar

Fry the coconut in the melted margarine until it turns a light golden colour. Immediately add in the porridgemeal and fry until it becomes a little crunchy. Sweeten with sugar. Sprinkle this mixture on top of stewed apples just before serving.

Shortcrust Pastry

Shortcrust pastry can be made using either the All-in-One **or** the Rub-In method. The water required can vary so use the quantities listed for the method you use. Only use the icing sugar in sweet shortcrust pastry. Wholemeal shortcrust pastry is made by the same methods.

Shortcrust (plain and sweet)

Flour	Icing Sugar (only for sweet)	Margarine	Water (All-in-One method)	Water (Rub-in method)
175 g (6 oz)	25 g (1 oz)	75 g (3 oz)	3 tablespoons	4 tablespoons
225 g (8 oz)	25 g (1 oz)	110 g (4 oz)	4 tablespoons	4 tablespoons
275 g (10 oz)	50 g (2 oz)	150 g (5 oz)	5 tablespoons	5 tablespoons
Wholemeal Shortcrust				
225 g (8 oz) { 110 g (4 oz) white flour **and** 110 g (4 oz) wholemeal flour		110 g (4 oz)	4 tablespoons	4 tablespoons
400 g (14 oz) { 200 g (7 oz) white flour **and** 200 g (7 oz) wholemeal flour		200 g (7 oz)	6 tablespoons	6 tablespons

[my tablespoon = 20 ml]

All-in-One method:
The margarine must be soft (not hard from the fridge). Put half the flour into a bowl with the sugar (if using it), the margarine and the water. Mix to a smooth paste using a fork or electric mixer. Then use fork only to mix in the remaining flour. Knead it by hand to make a smooth dough. This can be done in the bowl. Chill for 1/2 hour before using — except the wholemeal pastry. This can be used straightaway, which is very convenient. If chilled it is inclined to crack when rolled out.

Rub-in method:
For this method the margarine must be firm from the fridge. Put the flour into a bowl. Cut in the margarine in lumps and then rub it in until the mixture looks like fine breadcrumbs (a food processor will do this job in seconds.) Add just enough water to bind the dry ingredients together. Knead lightly and chill for $\frac{1}{2}$ hour — except wholemeal pastry, it is best to use this straightaway.

To Bake Pastry Case Empty ("Blind").

The All-in-One method of making pastry will result in pastry cases that hold their shape well when baked empty.

Never stretch pastry to fit, it will automatically shrink in the oven! Instead, roll it slightly larger and ease back in to tin. Chill empty pastry case well before baking. Pierce a few holes in the base and bake in a hot oven. **(200°C — 400°F — Gas 6)**. After about 5 minutes, open the oven door to check if the base of the pastry case is starting to rise up. If it is, pierce with a sharp knife to release the air!

Profiteroles (About 48 little choux puffs)

These make a most attractive dessert piled in a pyramid with the chocolate sauce dripping down. It is important to be accurate in the measurements for the choux pastry.

Choux pastry:
110 g (4 oz) flour
65 g (2½ oz) margarine
4 fresh eggs (medium — large)
150 ml (¼ pt) water
¼ teaspoon vanilla essence (see note)

Note: If the little choux puffs are going to be filled with a savoury filling — substitute the vanilla essence with salt and pepper.

To fill:
275 ml (½ pt) cream
Caster sugar to sweeten
2 teaspoons grated root ginger (optional)

Sieve the flour onto a piece of paper. Put the margarine (cut in lumps) into a saucepan with the water. Bring to the boil. Immediately add in all the flour. Stir mixture over a gentle heat for about 3-5 minutes. Take off heat and allow to cool.

Next beat in the first three eggs — one at a time, beating the mixture until smooth after each one. Add the vanilla essence at this stage. Break the 4th egg in a cup and add enough of it to the choux pastry to give the correct consistency, soft but yet stiff! Judge this by putting a spoon onto the surface of the pastry. Lift it off with a quick jerk so that the pastry underneath stands up in a little peak which should not flop sideways.

Put pastry into a piping bag with plain round nozzle and pipe in small blobs onto greased tin, **or** put out in teaspoonfuls. Bake in a hot oven (**200°C — 400°F — Gas 6**) for about 15-20 minutes until well risen, puffed and crisp. (Don't open oven door for first 10 minutes of baking.) When baked, pierce a hole the size of a large pea in the side of each puff. Return them to the oven for about 5-10 minutes to dry them out, this makes them nice and crisp. Cool on a wire tray.

Whip the cream, sweeten with caster sugar and flavour with the ginger. Fill the centre of the little choux puffs. Just before serving, cover with chocolate sauce.

Chocolate Sauce
Dark and Delicious

175 g (6 oz) dark chocolate
110 g (4 oz) sugar
275 ml (½pt) water
2 tablesp. red or blackcurrent jelly or jam
2 – 3 tablespoons brandy (optional)
3 tablespoons cream
1 level tablespoon cornflour

Break the chocolate into pieces. Put everything except the cream into a saucepan and cook over a gentle heat until sugar dissolves. Then bring to the boil. Simmer for 2 minutes. Add in cream. Blend the cornflour with a bit of little water. Add to the sauce, stir and bring to the boil, to thicken. Serve hot or cold.

Apple Tart

I like my apple tart to have a generous filling. Always chop the apples very small to ensure quick cooking.

Sweet shortcrust pastry using 275 g (10 oz) flour (page 78)

3 large cooking apples

2-3 tablespoons sugar

1 dessertspoon of flour

¼ teaspoon ground nutmeg.

Juice ½ orange

Tin: 23 cm (9″) sandwich tin or pie plate — greased.

Cooking time: about 35 — 45 minutes **(200°C — 400°F — Gas 6)** in upper half of oven.

Make the pastry. Divide unevenly in half! Use the larger bit to roll out and line the base of the tin. Roll out the other piece. Peel and finely chop the apples. Put them into a bowl with the sugar, flour and nutmeg, mix together and put into the base. Sprinkle with the orange juice. Cover the top with the remaining pastry. Wet the edges, press well to stick them together. Pierce a few holes in the top. Bake until the pastry is golden and the apples are tender. Test these by sticking a skewer through a hole in the pastry. Sprinkle a little caster sugar over the top before serving.

Chocolate Sponge

This is suitable as a dessert or as a cake. I like to bake it in a ring tin but it can also be baked in a deep cake tin.

75 g (3 oz) flour (see note)

25 g (1 oz) cocoa

4 large eggs

110 g (4 oz) caster sugar

60 ml (⅛ pt) water

¼ teaspoon vanilla essence

2 — 3 tablespons apricot jam or redcurrant jelly

Irish Mist or Baileys Irish Cream (optional)

Chocolate Cream:

110 g (4 oz) dark chocolate

60 ml (⅛ pt) water or fresh orange juice

250 ml (almost ½ pt) cream

Tin: Ring tin 24 cm (9½") diameter **or** 20.5 cm (8") cake tin. Grease the tin (place a circle of greaseproof in base of cake tin).

Cooking Time: About 40 minutes in ring tin **or** 1 hour in cake tin **(180°C — 350°F — Gas 4)**.

Sieve the flour and cocoa together onto a piece of paper. Separate the eggs, put the yolks into a bowl with the caster sugar, water and vanilla essence. Whisk until the mixture turns creamy. Stir in the sieved flour and cocoa. In a separate bowl, whisk the egg whites until stiff. Stir them through the egg yolk mixture, gently but thoroughly. Turn into the prepared tin and bake until the sponge springs back when pressed with a finger. Turn out onto wire tray to cool.

CHOCOLATE CREAM: Put the chocolate and water into a small saucepan and heat *gently* to melt it. Stir well. Allow to cool. Whip the cream and then stir in the chocolate. If you wish add a little "slosh" of Irish Mist.

To Assemble: Slit the sponge in two and sprinkle generously with Irish Mist **or** Baileys. Spread with the jam and a little of the chocolate cream. Sandwich together. Spoon the remaining chocolate cream over the top. Decorate with piped roses of whipped cream.

Note: If you are using an electric beater to beat the mixture, you will not need to use self raising flour as the air bubbles will be enough. Too much raising agent causes the sponge to collapse **or** shrink considerably when removed from the oven.

BREAD AND CAKES

Whenever I can, I like to use wholemeal flour in baking. Not only for its extra nutrition, but also because it is an excellent way to include fibre in the diet. The importance of cereal fibre is its ability to hold water which keeps our internal plumbing running nice and smoothly!

Brown Bread in a Casserole

Traditional brown bread plays an important role in my family's diet. I bake it in a casserole with the lid on. This keeps the steam in, which results in a well risen bread with a thin but crisp crust that has no cracks around the sides. I usually use a cast iron or a pyrex casserole but I have also successfully used a deep cake tin covered with an inverted sandwich tin. Whatever container you use must be heated in the oven beforehand until it is piping hot.

700 g (1½ lb) wholemeal flour
225 g (8 oz) flour (*or* use 450 g (1 lb) of each flour)
2 rounded teaspoons of bread soda
2 rounded teaspoons of baking powder
110 g (4 oz) raisins (optional — but rich in iron)
2 tablespoons oil
425 – 570 ml (¾ – 1 pt) buttermilk

Use 2.8 L (5 pt) casserole.
For a smaller bread, use half the ingredients and bake in a 1.75 L (3 pt) casserole.

Cooking time: 50—60 minutes (smaller 35—45 mins.) **(200°C — 400°F — Gas 6)** in upper half.

Put all the dry ingredients, including the raisins, into a bowl and mix thoroughly. Make a hollow in the centre and pour in the oil, immediately followed by three-quarters of the buttermilk. Mix with a wooden spoon and if necessary, add the extra milk to make a softish dough. Sprinkle some wholemeal flour in the base of the hot casserole and put in the dough. Sprinkle a little flour on the top and pat it down to smooth it. If you prefer, you can knead the dough first, on a floured surface. (I use a little tray that is easy to wash afterwards.) After kneading, turn up the smooth underside, shape into a round and place in the casserole.

Cut a cross over the surface of the dough. Cover with the lid and bake until well cooked. Avoid opening the lid for the first half hour of baking. When baked, turn onto wire tray to cool.

Short of buttermilk? Use fresh milk but substitute the bread soda with baking powder, (so you use 4 teaspoons all together). To give the bread its nice "soda" colour, mix in 1—2 teaspoons of treacle when adding the milk. By the way, treacle is rich in iron.

White Soda Bread

Substitute white flour for the wholemeal flour in the above recipe. Use self-raising flour and omit bread soda and baking powder. Use fresh milk not buttermilk.

Brown Scones

Make up half the brown bread mixture. Turn the dough out onto a floured surface. (Use the wholemeal flour to sprinkle on the surface.) Shape the dough into a square about 2.5 cm (1") thick. Divide into square scones with a knife about 5 cm × 5 cm (2" × 2"). Bake on a greased tin for about 25 minutes. **(190°C — 375°F — Gas 5)**. Cool on a wire tray.

Cheese Scones

Give your cheese scones that extra touch by brushing their tops with a little egg or milk and sprinkling them with sesame seeds.

450 g (1 lb) self raising flour
½ teaspoon of salt
Lots of freshly ground black pepper
50 g (2 oz) margarine (optional)
110 g (4 oz) grated cheese (red cheddar)
2 large eggs
Generous 150 ml (¼ pint) milk
Good teaspoon mustard

Cooking time: About 25 minutes **(200°C — 400°F — Gas 6)** on an upper shelf.

Note: I often substitute wholemeal flour for half of the self-raising flour and add a heaped teaspoon of baking powder.

Put the flour, salt and pepper into a bowl. Rub in the margarine until like bread-crumbs. Then mix in the grated cheese. In a separate container mix together the eggs, milk and mustard. Add enough liquid to the dry ingredients to make a softish dough.

Turn out onto a floured surface and divide in half. Knead each piece lightly, turn up smooth underside and shape into a circle about 2.5 cm (1") deep. Divide each circle into 4 to 6 scones. Bake on greased tins until well risen and golden brown.

Variation: A tablespoon each of chopped fresh parsley and fresh chives (if available) makes delightful green speckled Cheese and Herb Scones.

Stale scones come to life if cut in half and toasted.

Spicy Scones

The spices and fruit give a nice rich flavour to these scones.

450 g (1 lb) self raising flour
75 g (3 oz) caster sugar
110 g (4 oz) chopped mixed peel
75 g (3 oz) sultanas or raisins
1 teaspoon *each* ground nutmeg and cinnamon
2 eggs
2 tablespoons oil
150 ml (¼ pt) milk

Cooking time: 25—35 minutes **(200°C — 400°F — Gas 6)** upper shelf.

Mix together the flour, sugar, fruit and spices in a bowl. Whisk the eggs in a separate container and mix in the oil and the milk. Add the liquid ingredients to the dry ones to make a medium-soft dough. Turn dough out onto a floured surface. Knead lightly, turn up smooth underside and flatten out to about 2.5 cm (1") deep. Cut out scones with a cutter.

Bake on greased tins until well risen and golden brown. Cool on a wire tray.

Hot Cross Buns

The above scone mixture can also be used to make hot cross buns.

When dough is turned onto floured surface, divide it into 8—10 pieces and shape each one into a kind of ball. Place on greased tin with untidy bits tucked underneath. Flatten each one slightly and cut a cross on the top.

Bake as for scones.

To glaze: Brush with honey and return to oven for a few minutes to dry out.

Cool on a wire tray.

Tea Brack

There are many variations of this ever popular brack. I like to add a good teaspoonful of vanilla essence to the cold tea. Occasionally, I will also add a "slosh" of sherry or whiskey!

225 g (8 oz) *each* raisins and sultanas
110 g (4 oz) mixed peel
110 g (4 oz) brown sugar (or white)
275 ml (½ pt) cold black tea (or stout)
Small teaspoon vanilla essence
560 g (1¼ lbs) self raising flour
1 – 2 level teaspoons *each* ground nutmeg and cinnamon
50 – 110 g (2 – 4 oz) chopped walnuts (optional)
175 g (6 oz) margarine
2 large eggs, lightly beaten

Tin: 20.5 cm – 23 cm (8″ – 9″) round cake tin, well greased. Line base with greaseproof paper.

Cooking time: About 2 hours **(170°C – 325°F – Gas 3)** centre oven.

Put all the fruit (but not the walnuts) into a bowl. Add the sugar, tea and vanilla essence. Mix and leave to stand overnight.

Next day, put the flour, spices and walnuts into a bowl. Melt the margarine and while still quite hot, stir into the fruit mixture followed by the beaten eggs. Then stir the fruit mixture into the flour mixture, working quickly before the margarine cools and stiffens. Turn into the tin and smooth the top. Bake until cooked through, covering the top with foil when brown enough.

Alternative method: Instead of melting the margarine, rub it into the flour until like breadcrumbs and then add the spices and walnuts. Mix the eggs into the fruit mixture and stir into the flour mixture to make a softish dough, if necessary adding a little milk. Put in the tin and bake as above.

Cool in the tin standing it on a wire tray. Keep for a day or two before cutting.

To test if cooked, stick skewer into the centre. It should come out clean with no dough-like particles sticking to it.

Brownies

Rich chocolate squares, super for lunch boxes. They also make a great dessert if eaten hot with custard or cream. The wholemeal flour gives them an attractive crunchiness.

75 g (3 oz) self raising flour
75 g (3 oz) wholemeal flour
50 g (2 oz) cocoa
150 g (5 oz) margarine
225 g (8 oz) brown sugar (Demerara)
3 large eggs
1 medium cooking apple, grated
50 g (2 oz) chopped walnuts or peanuts raw

Tin: 20.5 (8″) square tin greased or lined.

Cooking time: About 1 hour 10 minutes **(180°C — 350°F — Gas 4)** centre shelf.

Mix the flours and cocoa together. In a separate bowl, beat together the margarine and sugar. Next beat in the eggs one at a time with a little bit of the flour mixture. Then stir in the remaining flour mixture. Finally, mix the grated apple and the nuts thoroughly through the mixture. Spoon into the tin, spread out evenly and bake in the centre of the oven. Partly cool in the tin, then turn out onto wire tray. Cut into squares.

Variation: 50 g (2 oz) raisins can also be included in mixture with walnuts.

Raisin and Nut Bars

I got this recipe from Australia. The honey and walnuts give a lovely flavour.

110 g (4 oz) margarine

50 g (2 oz) caster sugar

4 tablespoons honey 75 g (3 oz)

3 eggs

175 g (6 oz) self raising flour

A little milk if necessary

175 g (6 oz) raisins

110 g (4 oz) walnuts, chopped

Tin: Swiss roll tin 28 cm × 18 cm (11" × 7") **or** 23 cm (9") square well greased or lined.

Cooking time: About 35—40 minutes **(180°C — 350°F — Gas 4)** centre shelf.

Beat the margarine, caster sugar and honey together until soft. Beat in the eggs, one at a time with a little of the flour. Then stir in remaining flour. If dough is very stiff, add a tablespoon or two of milk. Stir in the raisins and walnuts. Spread mixture out in the prepared tin. Bake until a rich golden colour and the sponge springs back when pressed with the finger. Cool in the tin and then cut into fingers.

Honey helps keep cakes fresh longer. A handy way to weigh syrup or honey is to stand the full jar on the scales, note the weight and spoon out the amount required, by watching the scales.

Crunchy Chilled Chocolate Fingers

These are really rich and delicious. (Don't think of the calories!) No cooking is required.

300 g (11 oz) digestive biscuits

300 g (11 oz) dark chocolate

110 g (4 oz) butter

110 g (4 oz) caster sugar

50 g (2 oz) finely chopped almonds

50 g (2 oz) ground almonds (optional)

50 g (2 oz) raisins

50 g (2 oz) glacé cherries

1 tablespoon orange juice or brandy (optional)

Tin: 23 cm (9″) square tin, line base with piece of cling film or foil.

Finely crush the biscuits in a plastic bag using a rolling pin. (I find a food processor makes them too fine.) Melt the chocolate and butter in a bowl (standing in a saucepan of gently simmering water or on a defrost setting in microwave). Add in all other ingredients and mix well. Spread out evenly in prepared tin.

Chill thoroughly for a few hours and then cut into fingers.

Orange and Raisin Cake

The combination of raisins, walnuts and orange make this a tasty, light fruit cake.

225 g (8 oz) margarine

225 g (8 oz) caster sugar

4 eggs, large

350 g (12 oz) flour

110 g (4 oz) wholemeal flour

1 level teaspoon baking powder

Juice 2 oranges

225 g (8 oz) raisins

50 g (2 oz) walnuts, chopped

Tin: 20.5 cm (8″) round cake tin **or** long loaf tin 28 cm × 12.5 cm (11″ × 5″) well greased. Line the base with greaseproof paper.

Cooking time: About 1½—2 hours — round cake tin takes longest. **(180°C — 350°F — Gas 4)**.

Beat margarine and sugar until soft. Then beat in eggs one at a time, adding a little of the weighed flour. Mix flours and baking powder and stir into the mixture. Then stir in orange juice, raisins and walnuts. Spread out evenly in prepared tin.

Bake until cooked through, firm to the touch and a nice golden colour. Test the centre by sticking in a skewer. If it comes out without any dough-like particles stuck to it, it is cooked. Partly cool in the tin, then turn out onto wire tray to cool completely.

Glacé icing (not necessary at all but in case you take the notion!): Blend 6 tablespoons of icing sugar with a little fresh orange juice (to make it slightly runny) and spread on the cake.

Note: Use half the ingredients for a small loaf tin which will cook in about 1 hour.

Carrot Cake

Carrots, traditionally used as sweeteners in baking, give a lovely moist chewiness to this spicy flavoured cake. I like to use a ring tin for baking as it cooks quickly and is a great shape for slicing.

225 g (8 oz) self raising flour
110 g (4 oz) wholemeal flour
A generous teaspoon *each* ground nutmeg and cinnamon
1 level teaspoon baking powder
175 g (6 oz) margarine
110 g (4 oz) brown sugar
50 g (2 oz) honey or golden syrup
3 large eggs
350 g (12 oz) carrots, grated
Juice of 1 orange

Tin: 24 cm (9½") diameter ring tin **or** round cake tin 20.5 cm (8") diameter.

Cooking time: 1—1½ hours **(180°C — 350°F — Gas 4)** centre shelf.

Mix the flours, spices and baking powder together. In a separate bowl, beat together the margarine, sugar and honey. Beat in the eggs, one by one with a little of the prepared flour. Then stir in the remaining flour. Stir in the grated carrots and the orange juice. Spread out in the prepared tin.

Bake until cooked to a nice orange brown. Partly cool in tin and then turn out onto wire tray.

Variation: 50 g (2 oz) each raisins and mixed peel can be added with the grated carrots.

Cheesy Orange Icing

Normally I don't use any icing on the carrot cake, but you might like to try this one occasionally.

---

50 g (2 oz) cream cheese

50 g (2 oz) butter or margarine

2 tablespoons of orange juice

275 g (10 oz) icing sugar, sifted

Mix together all the ingredients and beat to a smooth paste — or buzz in the food processor. Spread over top of cake and decorate with slices of orange.

Cheesy Lemon Drizzle Cake

Sweetened fresh lemon juice is "drizzled" over the surface of the baked cake. The cornflour helps give a nice close texture to the sponge. Keep for a day or two before cutting. It freezes well. Serve in small slices.

---

110 g (4 oz) cream cheese

225 g (8 oz) margarine or butter

Grated rind and juice of 1 lemon

275 g (10 oz) caster sugar

3 large eggs

225 g (8 oz) self raising flour

50 g (2 oz) cornflour

50 g (2 oz) finely chopped almonds

Drizzle:

50 g (2 oz) caster sugar dissolved in the juice of 1 lemon

Tin: Ring tin 24 cm (9½") diameter **or** 20.5 cm (8") round cake tin, well greased.

Cooking time: About 1 hour — (longer in round cake tin). **(190°C — 375°F — Gas 5)**; after 30 minutes, reduce to **(180°C — 350°F — Gas 4)**.

Beat the cheese, margarine and lemon rind together and then beat in the sugar until the mixture is soft. Beat the eggs in, one at a time, with a little of the weighed flour. Sift the remaining flour and cornflour together and stir into the mixture with the lemon juice and the almonds. Spread out in the prepared tin. Bake until well cooked. The sponge rises up well in the ring tin.

Partly cool in the tin and then turn out onto a wire tray. Pierce cake with a fork and "drizzle" the sweetened lemon juice over the cake. When cold, ice it.

Lemon glacé icing:
Sieve about 175 g (6 oz) icing sugar and blend with fresh lemon juice to make it a little runny. Spread over top of cake and allow to dribble down the sides.

Note: Before icing, the cake can be split in two, then sandwiched back together with lemon curd.

Cider Fruit Cake

This is a great fruit cake. It is so easy to make and the fruit doesn't sink. It can be used as a Christmas cake. Do be sure to use the tin size recommended, because if put in a smaller tin the mixture will be too deep and so take far too long to cook.

560 g (1¼ lb) flour
1 level teaspoon *each* ground nutmeg, cinnamon and cloves
175 g (6 oz) butter or margarine
350 g (12 oz) brown sugar
450 g (1 lb) *each* sultanas and raisins
110 g (4 oz) mixed peel
110 g (4 oz) glacé cherries, chopped
110 g (4 oz) almonds, chopped
Grated rind and juice of 1 lemon
2 large eggs
1 mug (275 ml / ½ pt) cider
175 ml (6 fluid oz) milk
1 rounded teaspoon bread soda

Tin: 28 cm (11") square **or** 30.5 cm (12") round cake tin lined with double thickness of greaseproof paper.

Cooking time: About 2 hours **(180°C – 350°F – Gas 4).** Reduce heat, if necessary to 170°C – 325°F – Gas 3.

Sieve (or mix) the flour and spices into a bowl. Cut the butter in lumps and rub through the flour until like breadcrumbs. Mix the sugar, fruit, almonds and lemon rind in through the flour mixture.

In a separate bowl, whisk the eggs and stir in the lemon juice, cider, milk and the bread soda. Add the liquid ingredients to the dry ones to make a fairly wet mixture. Spoon into the prepared tin, spread out evenly and leave to stand overnight (or for 6—8 hours).

Bake until cooked right through (test with skewer). Cool cake in the tin, standing on a wire tray. Don't cut for a few days. This cake will keep 4-6 weeks, if kept in an airtight container.

Coconut 'n Oatmeal Biscuits *(About 16 biscuits)*

I just love the crisp crunchiness of these biscuits. They are very quick to prepare.

110 g (4 oz) desiccated coconut
175 g (6 oz) porridgemeal (rolled oats)
50 g (2 oz) flour
110 g (4 oz) caster sugar
150 g (5 oz) margarine
2 tablespoons water

Oven Temperature **(180°C — 350°F — Gas 4)**

Put all the dry ingredients into a bowl and mix together. Melt the margarine in a saucepan, as soon as it melts add in the water. Then pour this liquid into the dry ingredients and mix well.

Put tablespoonfuls of the mixture on greased baking tins. Flatten each one out to a biscuit shape about 0.5 cm (¼″) thick using a fork. Bake for about 15-20 minutes until a nice, pale, golden colour. Cool for a few minutes on the tin to allow them to stiffen, then lift gently onto a wire tray to cool completely.

CHRISTMAS

I like Christmas, I actually enjoy the fuss and the bother — winter would be long and monotonous without it. To keep the fuss at an enjoyable level, plan everything on paper. Do as much in advance as possible. Stick your list to the kitchen press so you can virtuously tick off each job as it is done!

Super Plum Pudding

The great thing about a pudding is that the fruit doesn't sink! Ideally, make it 2-3 months in advance so it will be nicely matured for Christmas. This one will actually keep for 12 months. The quantities I give are for 2 × 1.75 litres (3 pt) puddings. The amounts in the square brackets [ ] are for one pudding only.

Mixing Bowl 1:

450 g (1 lb) *each* **sultanas and raisins [225 g / 8 oz]**
450 g (1 lb) currants [225 g / 8 oz] (optional)
225 g (8 oz) *each* **glacé cherries and mixed peel [110 g / 4 oz]**
110 g (4 oz) *each* **figs and dates [50 g / 2 oz]**
110 g (4 oz) blanched almonds [50 g / 2 oz]
1 medium cooking apple [half]
Grated rind of 1 lemon [half]

Mixing Bowl 2:

225 g (8 oz) flour, white or wholemeal [110 g / 4 oz]
225 g (8 oz) breadcrumbs white or wholemeal [110 g / 4 oz]
110 g (4 oz) butter, margarine or suet [50 g / 2 oz]
225 g (8 oz) brown sugar [110 g / 4 oz]
1 generous teaspoon each of ground nutmeg, cinnamon and cloves [level teaspoon each.]

Mixing Bowl 3:

6 medium eggs [3]
275 ml (½ pt) stout [150 ml / ¼ pt.]
1 glass whiskey about 50 ml [½ glass / 25 ml]
Juice ½ lemon [½ a small lemon!]

Two pudding bowls 1.75 — 2 litres. (3-3½ pts) — well buttered inside.

Cooking time: Steam, boil or steam-bake for about 6 hours. A couple of days before eating — steam, boil or steam-bake for a further 1-2 hours.

Mixing Bowl 1: Chop the figs, dates, cherries and almonds. Peel and grate the apple and mix everything together.

Mixing Bowl 2: Put in the flour and rub in the margarine until the mixture resembles breadcrumbs. If using suet simply mix it in. Mix in the remaining ingredients.

Mixing Bowl 3: Whisk all the liquid ingredients together.

To Assemble: In a large basin, mix the contents of bowls 1 and 2 together. Then add the liquid from bowl 3 and stir thoroughly — making wishes! (One wish for every 3 stirs!) Divide the mixture between the two prepared pudding bowls and cover with a double layer of greaseproof paper. (This must be well greased and have a pleat/fold across the middle to allow for expansion). Tie the paper securely to the bowl with string. No paper is necessary if the bowl has its own lid.

To Steam
Stand the pudding bowl in the steamer and cover with the lid. The saucepan underneath must be checked constantly and topped up with boiling water when necessary. It is possible to boil the pudding in two 3 hour sessions if that is more convenient.

To Boil
Stand the pudding bowl in a saucepan on a scone cutter or a piece of wood (something to prevent it standing directly on the base of the saucepan). The water should come ¾ of the way up the sides of the bowl. Cover the saucepan with the lid, in such a way that some of the steam can escape. Top up with boiling water whenever necessary.

To Steam-Bake
Stand the pudding bowl in a large cake tin or a roasting tin. Fill it ¾ full of boiling water and cover generously with foil, tucking it under the sides of the tin to prevent steam escaping easily. Cook for about 6 hours in a slow oven **(150°C — 300°F — Gas 2).** Top up with boiling water when necessary.

To Store
Discard the wet greaseproof paper and re-cover with dry paper. Store in a cool airy place away from direct light. Do not store puddings in airtight containers/wrappings as this can cause them to go mouldy.

Brandy Butter

Don't forget the lemon juice, it gives a lovely "bite" to the flavour. This can be made a few days beforehand, then covered and stored in the fridge.

110 g (4 oz) butter or margarine
175 g (6 oz) caster sugar
2-4 tablespoons brandy or whiskey
1 tablespoon lemon juice

Cream the butter and sugar together and then beat in the brandy and lemon juice. Pile into a dish and chill.

Mincemeat

Use the **fruit listed in Mixing Bowl 1 of the pudding recipe.** Chop it all finely, or give it a quick "buzz" in the food processor (don't turn it into mush!) **Add 110 g (4 oz) suet, 1 teaspoon each of ground cinnamon, nutmeg and cloves, the juice of 1 orange and a glass of whiskey or brandy (50 mls) and 175 g (6 oz) brown sugar. Stir very well** and put into scrupulously clean jam jars. Cover with lid, (cling film or foil.) A pretty gingham cover transforms a jar into a present!

Rich Christmas Cake

The fruit is steeped overnight in a tin of strawberries. This makes the fruit deliciously plump and moist. The more fruit in a cake (or pudding) the longer it will keep because of the sugar in it. This cake will keep for at least 6 months. The amounts in the square brackets [ ] are for one cake only.

450 g (1 lb) *each* sultanas and raisins [225 g / 8 oz]
225 g (8 oz) *each* glacé cherries and mixed peel [110 g / 4 oz)
110 g (4 oz) figs [50 g / 2 oz]
50 g (2 oz) crystallized ginger [25 g / 1 oz]
1 medium cooking apple [half]
1 tin strawberries [½ tin], drained
Grated rind of 1 orange and 1 lemon [½ orange and ½ lemon]

About 3 tablespoons whiskey [1½]

110 g (4 oz) ground almonds [50 g / 2 oz]

110 g (4 oz) chopped almonds [50 g / 2 oz]

500 g (18 oz) flour, not self raising [250 g / 9 oz]

1 small teaspoon each ground nutmeg, cinnamon, and cloves.

450 g (1 lb) butter (or margarine) [225 g / 8 oz]

450 g (1 lb) brown sugar (demerara) [225 g /8 oz]

8 large eggs at room temperature [4].

Tins: 28 cm (11″) square tin **or** a 30.5 cm (12″) round cake tin. For the smaller cake — 20.5 cm (8″) square **or** 23 cm (9″) round tin.

The tins must be lined with a layer of brown paper and a double layer of grease-proof paper.

Cooking time: 1½ hours until cake has a set look, without being browned at **(170°C — 325°F — Gas 3)**. Reduce heat to **(150°C — 300°F — Gas 2)** and cook for a further 3-4 hours for larger cake and 2-3 hours for smaller one.

Ovens vary so it is necessary to use your own judgement. It is better to err on the side of a cooler rather than a hotter oven.

Chop the cherries, figs and crystallized ginger. Grate the apple and mix all the fruit in a bowl with the orange and lemon rinds, the drained tin of strawberries, and the whiskey. Leave to steep overnight to allow the fruit to soak up the juices. Just before using, stir in the ground and chopped almonds.

Sieve the flour and spices into a bowl together. In a separate bowl, cream the butter and sugar together until the mixture is soft — but don't overbeat. Beat in the eggs, one at at time, adding in a little of the flour with each one. When all the eggs are in the mixture, stir in the remaining flour. The cake mixture should be soft, but yet stiff enough so that it will only drop off a wooden spoon when it is shaken gently. (If necessary add an extra 25 g / 1 oz flour). Add the fruit mixture to the butter mixture and stir gently but thoroughly.

Spoon into the prepared tin and spread out evenly, making the surface slightly shallower in the centre (like a saucer).

Cover the tin loosely with a "lid" of brown paper or foil. Bake until cooked through, removing the "lid" for the last hour of cooking.

(Cont'd: next page)

Cool the cake in the tin (on a wire tray). Sprinkle the cake with more whiskey while it is still hot. When it is cold, wrap it in foil, place it in a plastic bag and store in a cool airy place. The occasional slosh of whiskey or brandy during storing doesn't do any harm!

Icing the Cake

ALMOND ICING

My problem is I check the flavour of the icing so much, I barely have enough left to cover the cake! This recipe makes enough for a 28 cm (11″) cake. (Use half for a 20.5 cm (8″) cake).

450 g (1 lb) ground almonds
275 g (10 oz) caster sugar
175 g (6 oz) icing sugar
2 small eggs
1½ tablespoons lemon juice
1 tablespoon of whiskey or brandy
½ teaspoon vanilla essence
½ teaspoon almond essence

Mix all the dry ingredients together. In a separate bowl, mix all the liquid ingredients together. Add the liquid to the dry ingredients to make a stiff moist paste. Gather the paste into a ball. Brush the top of the cake with softened apricot jam or a beaten egg white. Put the ball of icing on top and flatten it out until it covers the top of the cake. Smooth the surface with a rolling pin. I like my almond icing moist so I usually put the white icing on straightaway.

WHITE ICING

I use the instant royal icing which I pat into snow-like peaks, to decorate the cake! I colour some almond icing, green and some red and cut out candle shapes and holly leaves and arrange these on the top of the cake.

Once iced, I store the cake in a turkey roasting bag. This keeps the dust off and the moisture in — while allowing the cake to be seen!

Fruit 'n Nut Top

This looks very attractive and can be used instead of the white icing to decorate your almond icing.

Red and green glacé cherries
Blanched almonds
Walnut halves
Sliced crystallized ginger
Apricot glaze

Arrange the fruit and nuts in neat rows of contrasting colours, pressing them into the covering of almond icing. Brush with apricot glaze. (See cake in the front cover picture).

Apricot Glaze: Cook 2-3 tablespoons of apricot jam in a saucepan with the same amount of water until a nice thick consistency. Press through a sieve.

The Turkey

Once, I cooked my turkey in advance and reheated it on Christmas day. Never again. I was completely disorientated by the lack of delicious cooking smells!

If your are not over the moon about **the turkey legs,** you might like to cut them off and deal with them separately, (see Turkey Legs);

Removing the wish-bone before stuffing the turkey, makes the carving much easier. To remove it, first loosen the skin from the breast just around the neck area. Next, with your fingers, root along the edge of each breast at the neck cavity and locate the wish-bone. Loosen it as best you can with your fingers. Then use a small sharp knife or kitchen cutter to remove the stubborn sections.

Fill the neck cavity with the stuffing (page 102) and fold the skin right over, pinning it to the back with wooden cocktail sticks. I never stuff the body cavity of a turkey as it really slows down the cooking time. Instead, I put an apple, an onion, 1/2 lemon, thyme, bay leaf and parsley into the cavity to create moisture and flavour.

Weigh the stuffed turkey (with or without legs) and calculate the roasting time **or** add weight of made-up stuffing to weight of oven-ready turkey!

To Roast:
I like to roast the turkey in the traditional way starting in a hot oven **(220°C — 425°F — Gas 7)** for the first 30-60 minutes then reducing the heat to very moderate **(170°C — 325°F — Gas 3)** for the remainder of the time.

Approximate cooking times:
3·5 — 4·5 kg (8—10 lbs) 3-3½ hrs
4·5 — 6 kg (10—14 lbs) 3½-4 hrs
6—8 kg (14—18 lbs) 4-4½ hrs
8—9 kg (18—20 lbs) 5 hrs

(These times include the initial hot period in the oven)

It is important to spread the breast generously with butter or margarine or else cover it with slices of pork fat (which you can order from your butcher). Cover the turkey with a large piece of foil and baste occasionally as it roasts. Remove the foil (and pork fat) for the last 45 minutes of cooking to allow turkey to brown nicely. To check if turkey (with legs!) is cooked, use a couple of paper towels and squeeze the flesh on the thighs. It should be soft. A turkey without legs should cook in the allotted time as the breast is a much more tender meat.

TURKEY STUFFING

Sufficient to stuff the breast of a 4·5 — 6 kg (10 — 13 lb) oven-ready turkey.

1 large onion, finely chopped
50 g (2 oz) butter or margarine
225 g (8 oz) = 3 mugs fresh breadcrumbs, white or wholemeal
2 heaped tablespoons chopped parsley
2 teaspoons mixed herbs
Generous pinches ground nutmeg
Salt and freshly ground black pepper
Finely grated rind and juice of 1 lemon
3 sticks celery, finely chopped
450 g (1 lb) sausagemeat
About 150 ml (¼ pt) giblet stock (see note)
The chopped cooked turkey liver

Note: [Cook the turkey giblets (neck, liver etc.) in water with some vegetables and seasoning for about 45 minutes. Strain off the stock and chop the liver].

Fry the onion in the butter until soft. Then add all the ingredients into a bowl and mix thoroughly. If you would like to check the taste of the stuffing, fry a little blob of it on the pan to cook the sausagemeat. Do not stuff the turkey in advance.

TURKEY LEGS

Remove the bones from each leg of turkey. Your butcher will do this if you give him plenty of notice. It is easy enough to do it yourself with a sharp knife.

Cut through to the bone down the full length of the leg. Do this on the inside leg where the flesh is thinner. Gradually cut the flesh away from the bone. This is very easy except around the joint where you do the best you can! Then using a scissors cut away as many of the white stringy tendons as possible as these become very hard when cooked.

Spread out the boned leg meat, skin side down. Spread a little of the stuffing on top and roll up in a long sausage shape. Wrap tightly in microwave cling film (**or** hold in position by pinning with cocktail sticks. Then tie securely in quite a few places with fine string or cotton. Spread the rolls with butter and wrap in foil.) Place on the tin with the turkey allowing about 2 hours to cook. Remove foil for last half hour to brown.

Recipe suggestions for leftover turkey.
Turkey Risotto — page 15
Turkey Pie — page 25
Fruity Coleslaw — page 65

Boiled and Baked Ham

This is a handy way to cook ham. The boiling is done one day and the baking can be done on the following one.

The cooking method is the same for both pale and smoked ham. If you are using smoked ham, steep it overnight in cold water before cooking, so plan accordingly.

To Boil: Put the ham in a large pot and cover with cold water. Bring to the boil, pour off the water and cover again with fresh water. This time, add a collection of vegetables such as onion, carrot, celery and half a cooking apple to the water. Season with a little salt and plenty of freshly ground black pepper, also add some mixed herbs. Bring to the boil and simmer gently with lid on, allowing about 25 minutes for every 450 g (1 lb) ham, plus an extra 25 minutes at the end.

To Bake: The baking of the ham can be done the next day (if more convenient). Just leave the ham in the cooking water overnight. Reheat gently in the water before baking.

Lift the ham out of the water and remove the skin and as much of the fat as you like. Spread a layer of mustard all over the fatty side of the meat. Cover with a layer of brown sugar (demerara). Stick in about 15 whole cloves at random through the sugar. Put ham on a roasting tin and bake in a hot oven for about ¾ hour, basting occasionally until the sugar is well browned.

Recipe suggestions for Ham leftovers.

Quiche — use ham instead of rashers (don't fry), page 13.
Turkey Risotto — using ham instead of turkey, page 15.
Fruity Coleslaw — page 65.

> I always make sure to have buttermilk in the fridge at Christmas. On St. Stephen's Day, there is nothing to beat some freshly baked brown bread or scones!

Mulled Wine

Ideal for a winter party. Don't allow it to boil as all the alcohol will evaporate!

275 ml (½ pt) water
150 g (5 oz) caster sugar
1 thinly sliced lemon
4 whole cloves
1 level teaspoon cinnamon
1 litre red wine

Dissolve the sugar in the water over a gentle heat and then boil. Add in all the other ingredients and simmer gently until pleasantly hot. Cover and leave to infuse for 10 minutes.

Index

Conversion Tables

All these are approximate conversion, which have either been rounded up or down. Never mix metric and imperial measures in one recipe; stick to one system or the other.

Weights		Volume		Measurements	
½ oz	10g-15g	1 fl oz	25 ml	¼ inch	0.5 cm
1	25	2	50	½	1
1½	40	3	75	1	2·5
2	50	5 (¼ pint)	150	2	5
3	75	10 (½)	275	3	7·5
4	110	15 (¾)	425	4	10
5	150	1 pint	570	5	12·5
6	175	1¼	700	6	15
7	200	1½	900	7	18
8	225	1¾	1 litre	8	20·5
9	250	2	1·1	9	23
10	275	2¼	1·3	11	28
12	350	2½	1·4	12	30·5
13	375	2¾	1·6	**Oven temperatures**	
14	400	3	1·75	Mark 1 275°F	140°C
15	425	3¼	1·8	2 300	150
1 lb	450	3½	2	3 325	170
1¼	550	3¾	2·1	4 350	180
1½	700	4	2·3	5 375	190
2	900	5	2·8	6 400	200
3	1·4 kg	6	3·4	7 425	220
4	1·8	7	4·0	8 450	230
5	2·3	8 (1 gal)	4·5	9 475	240

	American		**Imperial**		**Metric**
Liquid	1 pt = 16 fluid oz	=	1 pt = 20 fluid oz	=	570 ml
	1 cup	=	8 fluid oz	=	225 ml
Chocolate	1 square	=	1 oz	=	25g
Flour	2 cups	=	1 lb	=	450g
Sugar	2½ cups	=	1 lb	=	450g
Butter	1 stick	=	4 oz	=	110g